Budapest

WALKS IN THE CITY
AN EXCURSION TO SZENTENDRE

WALKS IN THE CITY

FIRST WALK

1. Chain Bridge
2. Funicular
3. Royal Palace
4. Matthias Church
5. Fishermen's Bastion
6. Elizabeth Bridge
7. Rudas Bath
8. Statue of St. Gellért
9. Statue of Freedom
10. Citadel
11. Gellért Hotel and Baths

SECOND WALK

12. Houses of Parliament
13. Western Station
14. St. Stephen Basilica
15. Hungarian National Academy
    of Sciences
16. Redoute

17. Vörösmarty Square
18. Váci Street
19. Margaret Island

THIRD WALK

20. National Museum
21. Central Market Hall
22. Freedom Bridge
23. Synagogue
24. Opera House
25. Millenary Monument
26. Museum of Fine Arts
27. Art Gallery
28. Castle of Vajdahunyad
29. Széchenyi Bath

FOURTH WALK

30. Battyhány Square
31. King Bath

CONTENTS

anubius. This was the name given to the River Danube by the Romans, who worshipped this god. And, as is appropriate, for a "greatness" of Heaven, Danubius is responsible for all of the beauty Budapest is praised for.

Some million years ago the ancient Danube wound its way through the ring of mountains, where the town of Visegrád lies today, to slowly flood the area presently occupied by the Capital. This slow but living water deposited the sand and pebbles of faraway lands and heaped up hills which divided the river into hundreds of tributaries. Marshes were created on the right hand side. On the left side, the river's arrival marked end of the turbulent aeons of mountain-building activities that had lasted millions of years. The final result was fascinating; ditches and valleys criss-cross the serried range of medium sized mountains (300–500 metres high) and soaring cliff-tops, cradling the city in their richly wooded, picturesque embrace. This has produced a marvellous backdrop to the buildings.

Man, the builder, was also attracted to the Danube. This river, and the fault at the foot of the hills, where deep-earth hot springs have carved caves into the limestone. In living memory to this stand the famous thermal baths of the City, representing 1000 years of bathing culture. The first townsmen, following on the trail of the Roman legions, built Aquincum in the present day Óbuda. They also used the River as a guideline, choosing its narrowest stretch with many fords.

The old Danube is still the main axis of the highly populated City. The busy main roads can trace their origins back 1000 years to the original roads and the old East-West Danube crossing via the Pest Buda ferry. The avenues of Pest lead to the main roads once marked by the City gates. They are all spokes of the ancient Great Boulevards' arcs. The inner arc—today's Vámház körút, Múzeum körút, Károly körút plus Deák Ferenc Street—follows the outer perimeter of the once existing walls and touches the Danube at both ends. The second arc was built much later, about hundred years ago, and is known as the arc of the Nagykörút (Great Boulevard). The third, unfinished but clearly visible crescent is the section of the Hungária körút, which is also in keeping with the tradition of the city structure. On the left, in Buda, a similar network of two concentric semi-circles, segmented by avenues, mirrors the roads on the opposite side of the river, despite Buda's uneven terrain. The disposition of roads leaving Buda is determined by the geography of the land. This almost musical rhythm is completed with the axis of the Danube and its panoramic view. The river is wide enough to allow probing eyes to range freely across to the opposite shore, but is not so wide as to limit a detailed view. There is a unique balance in the picture, as if some great composer had created all of its elements, even the ones formed millions of years ago. The inner parts of this "spider-web" structure are densely built, and as we go away from the Danube, the scene changes to a more spacious one.

Of course the City not only has an urban history; the chronicle of this physical order is also connected with its other history. The first important year in the life of Budapest is 106 AD, when the Roman town of Aquincum, which had already existed for decades, became the capital of Pannonia Inferior. After a further eighty years the Empire began to extend its territory to the left bank of the Danube. Around 190 AD the *castrum* was built, as one of the fortifications of the boundaries, which later became the core of medieval Pest.

At about 400 AD there was a large upheaval, barbaric tribes set Aquincum on fire and razed it to the ground. After a further hundred years the Eastern Goths and other East-Germanic tribes, the Lombards, the Avars, and the Francs were carving up the land between themselves and fighting against Attila and his Huns, as well as each other, for control of the areas of Pest, Buda and Óbuda. They made no improvements to the city, only accepting and occupying the old one.

The decade of the Hungarians' conquest from 890 brought the first change on the Buda side, around the shallow fords. After two and a half hundred years Pest had been born, and it is under this name that it received its first charter as a town from the King Béla IV.

These are the years following the Tartars ravages—the Mongols of Batu and Ghengis Khan destroyed the country in two long campaigns—but this was also the birth of the present city. The king built a fortress in Buda on the hill, Pest was expanding and Margaret Island had been occupied and built up by the newly organised ecclesiastic communities. Óbuda, the grey little village was also about to change; at the end of the XIII. century a parliament was held there, and from then on it was called the "Queen's Town". The ever present queens acquired land, houses and other benefits here.

The rank, position and growth rate of the three settlements changed from time to time, but their overall development was unbroken until the middle of the XVI. century, when the Turks, with their hopes of world domination arrived and inhabited the Capital for exactly 150 years. The Turks didn't build. They lived in both Buda and Pest, taking away the decaying palace's stones in order to construct some form of weak shelters.

When the liberating united Christian armies of Europe expelled the Moslems, there was hardly anything left of the medieval towns, and nothing of the famed splendour built during the kingship of the great Matthias. Following this, the architectural chronology started again, and continued steadily until the middle of the XIX. century. At that time (from the years of the 1830's, but in some districts from the turn of the XVIII. century), the neo-classical style was dominant, incorporating the new style for the palaces. Pest and Buda shaped into modern cities under its influence, and prepared for the year of the grand change when the old dream was to be fulfilled, that they join together with Óbuda to become one metropolis.

Budapest, as the capital of Hungary, a much bigger Hungary than the present one, was officially born in 1873, at which time there were in total 300.000 people inhabiting both sides of the river. The union triggered a rapid period of development. The rushed (built almost at American speed) buildings, the spectacular growth of the population (in 1896 there were 600.000 inhabitants, double that of the previous quarter of a century) once more changed the face of the city. The neo-renaissance mansions, the rows of Hungarian art nouveau buildings, mixed with some neo-classicism, created a metropolis with a homogeneous face on both sides of the Danube, especially on the faster growing Pest side.

The face of the city had been formed by the turn of the XX. century. Although it was partially destroyed by the Second World War (Budapest was a seat of military operations again in 1944–45), every reconstruction that has taken place since then has reached back, taking samples from its heydays; the basic structure of which has remained to this day. Within the town's appearance flourishes the era of the monarchy, the most beautiful years of Hungary with all of its memories. There are also the monuments commemorating Hungary's foundation a thousand years ago, which were built by 1896, the huge anniversary of the millennium celebrations. In the light of all these, the modern day architectural contributions do not say very much to us when looking around the City. However it says more of its citizens living within the ring of "sleeping" towns built between 1950–1980 in the huge densely packed blocks of flats, which surround the old inner core with a choking embrace.

Budapest, born by the end of the 1800's, then brand new and as pompous as Vienna, has recently celebrated its one hundredth birthday. This Budapest can be seen everywhere in the City, staying inside the third circle, of course. This is Budapest today. The way the tourists love and praise it.

An enchanting city with palaces, set in the womb of the hills with a backdrop from a fairy tale and the Danube flowing with grace in the middle. Danubius, called Ister in the Roman myths, is the one we can thank for the whole story.

First walk

CASTLE OF BUDA ◆ TABÁN ◆ GELLÉRT HILL

The stubby Castle Hill (Várhegy) and its neighbour the rough, romantic limestone giant, the Gellért Hill (named after the bishop who christened the pagan Magyars) and the ridge of the hill lying between them the Tabán, together with the narrow stretch of the Danube bank, have been populated since ancient times. The thermal waters wound their way through the Castle Hill's body and created countless caves which the hunter gatherer people at the dawn of civilisation used for shelter. On the slopes of the Gellért Hill the Eraviscuses held forth their culture, and the temple of their gods was probably situated where the Citadel now stands. This Celtic tribe was swallowed without a trace by the mixed population who followed the Roman legions and built the town of Aquincum.

Henceforth the history of this area continues steadily from the kings of the Middle Ages to the present day. The first fortress had been built in the XII. century on the Castle Hill, and its servants, together with their families were allowed to build little huts around it. This little village and the fortress formed the foundation of the proud Buda; the heart of this historical capital of Hungary. This ancient town preserving the past in its carved stones, and its younger sister, Pest had been already connected since the early 1800's, but were prevented from uniting by the lack of a permanent bridge over the Danube. The construction of a bridge had been undertaken

The legendary lion of the Chain Bridge

by the "Greatest Hungarian", Count István Széchenyi, the champion of national ambitions, state reforms and modernisation. We are now standing at the abutment of this one hundred and fifty year old bridge on the Buda side. The starting point of our first tour is at this bridge, significant in representing the present

face of Budapest and symbolic of the self esteem of the nation.

The foundation stone of the **Chain Bridge (Lánchíd)** was placed into the Danube's bed in 1842 and the bridge was opened to traffic seven years later, in 1849. The Chain Bridge was one of the wonders of the Earth at that time. Its only parallel could be found in London, which is where the design comes from originally. The structure designed by William Thierney Clark, hangs from huge metal chains. It wouldn't have been wise to block the path of the winter ice with many pillars and so this pre-requisite led to the choice of a remarkable piece of engineering. Construction was precisely carried out using products from the Hungarian metal works.

The first permanent Pest-Buda bridge formed the only crossing for a long distance along the banks. The next nearest steady bridge was to

The Chain Bridge

be found as far away as Vienna, and consequently it was of great importance to the organisation of the country and its economy. With its cast iron ornaments, its structure radiating calm dignity and balance, it is one of the finest industrial monuments in Europe. There is a story about the Chain Bridge, which is probably the most famous in Budapest folklore. It is said, that during the ceremony of the dedication of the Chain Bridge, a cobbler's apprentice noticed that the sculptor, János Marsalkó had forgotten to carve the tongue of the lions. He made a loud statement of his discovery and the artist apparently committed suicide out of shame by jumping into the Danube. Of course not a word of the story is true. Our sculptor in fact lived until an old age and the lions have tongues. They don't stick

9

out, as they are lions and not dogs panting in the heat said Marsalkó, who also had the fortune to hear this story several times.

The Chain Bridge which we have just looked at, even the first pillar, is not the original one that was opened to the public and the cobbler's apprentice in 1849. The famously beautiful structure was destroyed, as were all the bridges of Budapest during the bombings of the Second World War. However this version is an exact replica of the original one.

From the bridge abutment we can go either left or right along the roads that run parallel to the river to discover the "ground floor" of Buda.

It is possible to go straight on through the tunnel, although this is not recommended on foot nowadays. For example the keeper of the bridge will never again step out on to the

The Funicular and the Tunnel

10

balcony of his flat built into the gateway of the tunnel as he would probably die from the fumes...

However we go neither left, right, nor straight on. Our way leads upwards, onto the entrance square of the castle. Let's stay for a moment to look at the **Tunnel (budai közúti alagút)** once more. It joined the little villages behind the hill to the Capital after it was built between 1853 and 1857. Like William Clark, the constructor and building manager, Adam Clark, was also English, though not of the same family. He stayed in Hungary after finishing the work and lived in Fő Street, near his place of work. The total length of the tunnel is 350 metres, the height at the gates reaches 10 metres. The classical gateway overlooking Pest is especially nice, it is embellished with the old Hungarian coat of arms.

The same **coat of arms** can be seen (the complete heraldic version) on the wall next to the Funicular. This lavish mosaic was put together more than a hundred years ago from

The historical coat of arms of Hungary

The Tunnel's entrance facing the Danube

coloured, glittering stones, but it was walled up for forty years as it wasn't politically correct to picture angels in Hungary between 1948 and 1989. It's restoration occurred in the early nineties.

We start our journey up to the Castle by a strange elevator (long ago our predecessors gave the name "Castle" to the whole ancient Castle district). The **Funicular (Sikló)** was opened to the public in the 1860's and was rebuilt in 1986. It was steam powered and employed a clever trick; utilising the weight of

11

The lower station of the Funicular

the passengers and car going downwards to help pull the one coming up. The cars illustrate the splendid taste of the craftsmen of the XIX. century. While riding the cars, a wonderful panoramic view of Pest can be enjoyed.

As we step out of the Funicular's hall at the top, we can see the buildings of the former King's Palace to the left, and some rows of streets occupying the narrow plateau of Castle Hill to the right. There is the Saint George Square in front of us, which used to be of greater importance in the Middle Ages. Here lay the official and natural boundary between the king's and the public's Buda, a deep ditch carved by the thermal waters into the limestone, reinforced by a great stone wall. At the west edge of the square there are still excavations going on, as there are to the north where the Hungarian Defence Ministry once stood above the ruins of an early church.

We start our walk in the Bourgeois District. The first building we look at is the **Alexander Palace (Sándor Palota)**. It was built in 1806 and was the work of one of the most famous Pest-Buda architects, Mihály Pollack. His typical style is shown by the grand reliefs standing in the middle of the first floor's façade. The figures were made by the Bavarian Anton Kirchmayer. It was built as a private palace, but only two generations of the Sándors lived in it. From 1865 to 1945 it was used as the office of the Hungarian Prime Minister. After its renovation it is going to be a museum. During the excavations a fantastic construction was found under the courtyard and the cellars. This was a giant well sealed "funnel", an artificial hole, which led the waters from all directions into the middle, from where the monks, who had a friary here in the centuries before the Turks' invasion, could have scooped it out. Such a clever, well planned and probably efficient design has not yet been found anywhere else in Europe.

On the next site stands the charming building of the **Castle Theatre (Várszínház)**. It was finished between 1725 and 1736 and was used as a Carmelite chapel. Before that, in the Middle Ages, it served as a Franciscan church. After the dissolution of many monasteries, including this one, by Emperor Joseph II. the building was converted into a playhouse by the genius Farkas Kempelen, who was the inventor of the world famous chess-automaton. This was the Capital's first permanent stone theatre. It was opened more than two hundred years ago, on 17th October, 1787. Perhaps the biggest event in its long history occurred on 7th May, 1800, when the reigning prince of music, Ludwig van Beethoven gave a concert to the dignified inhabitants of Buda who have arrived in lavish coaches. Moving forward down the Theatre

The Alexander Palace

Street, we can find the **Carmelite Order's monastery (Karmelita rendház)**. It was extended and rebuilt in the XIX. century in the classical style. Previously, as the Theatre, it demonstrated features of the late baroque plaited style. The XVIII. century's frescos of the former refectory on the ground floor were recently restored.

There is an especially charming part of the **Castle Promenade (Vársétány)** behind the building. Rows of gas-lights illuminate the arc of the path until the Funicular, giving a romantic atmosphere on quiet summer nights. From here we can look down onto the most important artery of the district, a serpentine which leads from the tunnel up to the Dísz

13

A romantic part of the Castle Promenade

district. On the northern side of the square stands a **monument commemorating the soldiers of the War of Independence (magyar honvédhısök emlékszobra)**. In 1848–49 Hungary was fighting for its independence from the Austrian Emperor. One of the many small victories in this lost war occurred when the Hungarian solders won the Buda Castle in a battle in 1849.

The square is surrounded by baroque, neo-classical and eclectic dwellings. They were mostly built after the liberation from the Turks at the end of the 1600's and the beginning of the 1700's. Many of them were erected on medieval foundations and include medieval wall fragments. These styles summarise the historical and architectural feature of the whole district. The slowly burgeoning, sometimes dignified inhabitants of the district were subsequently building mansions from the 1400's, which had been unmaintained by the four-five generations of Turks. The liberation of Buda in 1686 started a new age and over the period of several decades the baroque Castle district was built. At the beginning of the XIX. century the palaces were rebuilt in the classical style, mostly in harmony with those built two hundred years before. After the bombing and house-to-house street-fighting of the Second World War the task of rebuilding was not trivial. At places the reconstruction reaches back to the baroque, sometimes to the classical stage, or to neither at all, building something totally new. That is why you get the impression when walking in the citizens' district that you are walking in a museum of architecture.

4–5. Dísz Square, also built in the years right after the liberation using the walls of its medieval predecessor, was a property of the **Kremsmünster Monastery**. The only features that preserve the essence of that time are the ground floor façades and the recessed benches, called *sedilia*. The so-called **Passardy House**

Square nearby. You can just make out the shape of the gate that once stood here (a single column and the trace of the pillars supporting the arches). This is known as the **Vizikapu (Water Gate)**, earlier called the **Saint John Gate**, where the person arriving would have been stopped by soldiers armed with halberds. The **Dísz tér (Parade Square)** got its name from the military parades held in front of the ugly Second World War ruins of the Head of Defence Palace. Here is the southern gate of the citizens'

The western row of houses on the Dísz Square

(11. Dísz Sq.) fell into the hands of the wealthy John Passardy in 1711. The neo-baroque gate surround had been built one hundred years earlier, in 1620, when the reconstruction of the façade in classical style started.

13. Dísz Square, the Salgáry House preserved some features of the building which stood in its place during the pre-Turkish period. The first section of the entrance is from medieval times, and is barrel-vaulted. The stairway and the façade are in classical style, the result of a reconstruction in 1815, together with the proud lion-headed gate and the ornaments in relief above the first floor windows, that of Diana, Rea Sylvia praying for Romolus and Remus, and Athena. Within this building for a long time operated one of the oldest chemists of the area.

The courtyard of 15. Dísz Square

As far back as 1768 John Kajetan Beer was selling his products here.

Probably the house on **15. Dísz Square** preserved the greatest proportion of baroque architecture in the area. The wing facing the square was built in the 1720's. Its bright, arcaded courtyard, which is closed by the castle wall, is itself a real beauty.

We now travel along the **Úri utca (Gentlemanly Street)** northwards. This is the only row of houses which runs in the north-south direction in this area. Although the façades do not, the courtyards, the ground floors, the gateways with their recessed benches, the cellars, with long since dried up wells, all bring back the forgotten atmosphere of rich medieval Buda. From the iron gate of **No 9. Úri Street** a flight of steps leads three stories deep below the hill into the labyrinth of the **Castle Caves (budai várbarlangok)**. Moving on, with a little help from our imagination we can travel through time. These cellars and caves (natural caves carved by the waters and joined together by men) form a multi-leveled network under the entire district. Archaeological findings tell us that many of the passages are five to seven hundred years old. Only a small section of the cave-system can be visited, where the blood-curdling exhibits of the **Wax Museum** help to bring back to life the lost medieval centuries. When we continue our journey once again under the blue sky, we can choose an easy walk. We can peer into the courtyards, taking a glimpse at the only Gothic, and two-story(!) dwelling at **No. 31**, or the remains of the lived-in-tower **(No. 37)** dated to the early Middle Ages, and almost totally hidden by other buildings. In this area is the **Balta-köz (Hatchet-close),** which joins Úri Street with Tárnok Street with a narrow alley. There are three ancient trades houses standing next to each other, **14. 16. and 18. Tárnok Street**. Two of them present the passer-by with an

unusually formed arcade with their first floors sticking out and supported by stone columns. The wall frescos of No. 14 are also from the XV. century. No. 18 used to house the other old chemist from 1745. It was called "To the Golden Eagle". Nowadays it houses the **Museum of Pharmacy (Patikamúzeum)**. There is a beautiful Madonna sculpture by the famous Hungarian ceramic artist, Margit Kovács in the façade's niche. Walking on, we take a look at 750 year old sedilas with pointed arches at the south wall of the courtyard in **Veszprémi House (38. Úri Street)**, the remains of the XV. century wall and gate behind **41. Úri Street**, which are the oldest built relics of the district. The splendid baroque house built around 1720, is the **Hadik House, No. 58.** In modern times it is

Old houses of merchants in Tárnok Street

still used for festive occasions such as weddings. Slowly we get to the northern end of the street, where a huge monstrosity lies; **No. 49**, the many winged building. After the conquest of Buda, the nuns and Franciscan monks built their churches and cloisters in this area. After the dissolution of the orders at the end of the 1780's, the Imperial Lieutenancy Council moved into these buildings, following their conversion to this use. Also within the scope of these changes was the **Parliament of Buda** built in 1784 with the entrance under **28. Országház utca (Parliament Street)**. Its stairway and celebration hall, being especially rich in

58. Úri Street

ornaments of the plaited style deserve special attention. At present it is used by the Hungarian Academy of Sciences as a congress building. At the end of the street, but adjoining the Kapisztrán Square stands the **Church of Mary Magdalene (Mária-Magdolna templom),** with its huge coarse tower representing the medieval style. It already stood out emphatically in 1496, and even before then there used to be a church in its place, which was given to the Observant monks by Béla IV. He was the king who "created" Buda, who re-established the state after the Mongols' invasion and built the protective stone fortresses, including Buda, all over the country. The late medieval descendant

was destroyed in the Second World War. Where once its nave stood is now a "garden of ruins", showing the remains of the different periods' stone buildings, guarded by a richly moulded great window which was rebuilt. The place we just arrived at used to be the market of the citizens in the Middle Ages. We will make a small detour turning to the left, for the sake of a view of a section of Budapest's panorama, which, probably we would have otherwise missed during our walks around the town. There is another large block in the north-west, which used to be the **Nándor-barracks.** Its first sections were built in the early 1700's, then it was reshaped and widened three times

38. Úri Street

in the XIX. century. Today's character can be described as puritan classicism. In front of the main entrance stands a wreath of gleaming cannons; the building is used as the **Museum of Military History** and also for archives. Beyond the parapet to the north-west the view stretches to the crescent of hills overlooking the city with their protective embrace. Here the wall breaks and opens a gap allowing the eye to freely traverse across the landscape. The **János-hegy (John Hill)**, crowned by the hundred year old brilliant white circular lookout tower, serves as a convenient orientation point. To the left of the János-hegy stand a range of hills; **Széchenyi-hegy**, **Sas-hegy**, **Gellérthegy** and to the right it includes the **Hárshegy** and **Remetehegy.**

We now continue our walk in an easterly direction along the tree lined promenade until the next gap in the wall, where the white stones of a strange tomb are gleaming. This is the **monument to Abdurrahman (Abdurrahman monumentuma)**, the last Turkish pasha, who fought like a lion, even though he was in his seventies, in the reconquest of Buda, over three hundred years ago. However the Turkish Buda couldn't withstand the combined forces of the European Christian Army. The pasha himself was mortally wounded in the ensuing battle. He refused to flee, preferring death to retreat.

A few more steps uphill, and we are at the top of the Bécsi kapu (Vienna's Gate), with the most enclosed square in the district before us. The neo-Gothic building on the right is home to the **National Archives (Országos Levéltár)**, where it is worth taking a closer look at its ceremonial stairway and the lead glass windows). Táncsics Street opens onto this square, towards which we are now heading.

The **Bécsi kapu (Vienna's Gate)**, a faithful reproduction of the original town gate opens the second busiest road onto the square. There are charming baroque, braided and

The Mary Magdalene Church

19

Old cannons in the courtyard of the National Army History Museum

pre-classical town houses around the square. The façade of **No. 7**, clearly visible from our vantage point on top of the gate is decorated with neo-classical medallion-shaped reliefs of Vergil, Socrates, Quintilan and Seneca. The house was built in 1807 and belonged to Grigely József, professor of literature and Latin. **1. Bécsikapu Square** was built around 1795 and **No. 5** around 1780. The latter of which also illustrates the braided style in its stairway and the railed pendant corridor. This is a delight for the traveller attracted to detail. **No. 6**, built around 1730, mixes the previous styles with that of the baroque, but it also kept the Gothic wall pieces in its façade. The Saint John of Nepumuk statue is an engaging ornament standing in the niche between the first floor windows.

No. 8 was the most recent dwelling to be built. Its style was that of the 1820s, contemporaneous with its construction, although the wing, overlooking Kardos Street and the gateway are in medieval late Gothic style. With its early classical style this house stands out in the row, but only for those who are expert in the history of architecture. For the rest of us it looks as charming as the rest of the buildings on the square. It has a special addition, an ancient vine-stock, which was a young sprout at the beginning of the 1800s. The entire courtyard is netted with the huge vines of Vitis Labrusca, this strong American Isabelle-type vine.

We turn back to the Dísz Square, passing the 100 year old evangelist church standing on the corner of Táncsics Mihály Street. This is one of the oldest streets of the district. It was called the street of Jews in the Middle Ages. Here stood their great synagogue and their houses, among which we can spy individual baroque restoration as we walk by. **No. 23 Táncsics**

▷ *The building of the National Archives*

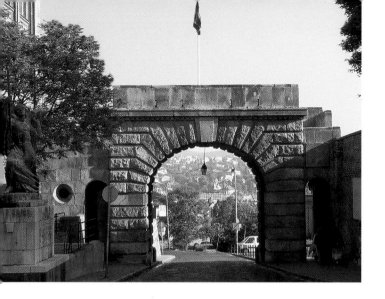

The Vienna Gate

Mihály Street, built in 1745 is an example of this. In the courtyard and its wall uses many roman stones, baroque sculptures, the remains of the once famous Almássy-collection. The gates themselves of **No. 18**, built in 1720, deserve special attention. Its neighbour of the same age has a remarkable addition, the stucco framed fresco between the first floor windows of Christ, the Virgin Mary and the saints.

The former Joseph-barracks of **No. 9** were built later, at around 1810. Of course it has much earlier predecessors. According to some, there previously stood a XIII. century fortress and castle, that of Béla IV., known as the Great Royal Mansion, later becoming the **Kammerhof (Royal Court of Justice)**. The proponents of this theory say this king, the "rebuilder" of the country, didn't have his court on the southern end of the hill, where the castle now stands, but instead here, in the middle of Táncsics Street. The prison of the Austrian **Regent's Council** operated here for a long time and many legendary heroes fighting for independence, from Lajos Kossuth to Táncsics Mihály, have been imprisoned here. A plaque on the wall in relief commemorates these events.

No. 7 Táncsics Mihály Street, the **Erdődy**

House, is probably the nicest baroque house in the district. Today only its façade shows its history. It was built around 1750. Beethoven stayed here during the time of his guest performance in the spring of 1800. The courtyard, perhaps in remembrance of this important episode, is the setting for intimate summer concerts.

The street we have been walking along now opens into a garland of squares. The first was named after András Hess, who produced the first printed matter in Hungary, the Chronicle of Buda in the year of 1437. Here, on this square stands the **Red Hedgehog House.** Its gate and

The picturesque baroque houses of Bécsikapu Square

built in the XVIII. century with its rich braided style. Apart from the extraordinary site of the Hilton Hotel, the exceptional architectural design is the reason this hotel is considered to be the most beautiful in the chain. Further to the south is the **Trinity (Szentháromság) Square**. The carved baroque statue was erected as a thanks-giving memorial by the survivors of a plague epidemic at the end of the 1700s. Residing on the square is the former **Town Hall** with a **statue of Athena the patroness of the**

... and its courtyard

23. Táncsics Mihály Street ...

coat of arms are dated 1820. It used to be a well known inn at that time, but the house was here already in the XV. century, the rooms on the ground floor show the remains of the medieval style.

Opposite the Red Hedgehog another present-day inn mirrors the old world in its façade. This is the **Hilton Hotel**. If we could say this absolutely modern building is without predecessors, then we would not be in Buda. The hotel's designers incorporated into its fabric ancient remains still present on the site. The result is a fascinating syntheses of old and new architectural elements. Included in the medieval remains are the tower of the **Church of St. Nicholas** in the outside wall, and the rearranged stone ornaments of the nave of the former **Dominican Church**. Looking out from its interior one can admire the panorama of Pest across the river. Other skilful inclusions are the ambulatory of the Dominican Cloister and the remains of the medieval **Jesuit College**,

7. Táncsics Mihály Street

city placed on one of its corners. This is the work of an Italian sculptor who hoped to obtain the much coveted citizenship of Buda in exchange for his work at this time. The Italian styled baroque Town Hall was built in the 1690s using old Gothic walls to the plans of Venerio Ceresola. It functioned as Buda's Magistrate's Office from 1710 until the union in 1873.

On the east side of the square rises the magnificent **Matthias Church (Mátyás templom)**. Dating back to the early Middle Ages, it was rebuilt by 1896. This church is a sacred place for Hungarians. It used to play an important role in the nation's history as the church for coronations. Its significance, in addition, is due to its pleasant setting and the variety if its long and turbulent history. Visitors can usually enter the church through the Maria Gate, the southern gate behind the tower. The interior is neo-Gothic, the cosy dimness brings back the atmosphere of the nave in medieval times. It was decorated by the most famous Hungarian historical painter of the XIX. century, Bertalan Székely. The wall-paintings and coloured windows are Székely's, and the greatest fresco-painter's, Károly Lotz's, work. The remains of Béla III. (reigned 1173–1198) and his French Queen, Anne of Chatillon have lain here since 1898, when they were brought from Székesfehérvár, where coronations were held in the Middle Ages. The Treasury with its exceptionally beautiful lithurgic accessories, made from old, noble materials, can also be visited. The so-called Matthias-chalice exhibited here is from the Middle Ages and worth a fortune. You can also find here an exact copy of the Black Madonna from the Italian Loretto, made in XVII. century.

When the richly moulded "wedding dress" construction of the Matthias Church was rebuilt

The Town Hall of Buda behind the statue of Captain Hadik

The Hilton Hotel, a meeting of old and new

by the end of the XIX. century, a worthy setting was immediately sought. By 1901 the bulky, old, grey walled **Fishermen's Bastion (Halászbástya)** was given a new silhouette, with its many little turrets, parapets, and stairways, designed by Frigyes Schulek, who had redesigned the Church. It was and still is a main attraction for tourists and plays an important role in shaping the face of Budapest. Framed in the arches of the Fishermen's Bastion stands Alajos Strobl's **statue of St Stephen (Szent István)**, Hungary's first king, carved in 1906. In the relief around the base of the statue, the sculptor himself can be recognised as the

◁ Trinity Square with the Matthias Church

The main nave of the Matthias Church

The stone laced tower of the Church

bearded gentleman offering the miniature of the church to the king.

From above, standing by the parapet of the Bastion we feel as if we can almost touch the living city below, seemingly only a few metres away. The spider web structure of the roads and the bridges connecting the arches are clearly visible. Church spires protrude from the thick texture of the City. To the left Margaret Island appears, like some stocky green surfer. Let's

The Fishermen's Bastion

spend a short fifteen minutes here and try to get our bearings. Tomorrow or the day after we will look more closely at some of its features. Walking down the marble steps of the Fishermen's Bastion we approach the János Hunyadi Street, along which we will continue our journey. Another five minutes and we reach the Water Gate, through which we enter the Castle. The Dísz Square is in front of us, to the left is the Színház Street with the Funicular at its end. Five more minutes and we are at the **Triumphal Arch of the Castle wing (palotaszárny díszkapuja)**. The ancient Hungarian totem, the huge statue of the proud turul bird, resembling the golden eagle, quivers with the sword of valour in its claws above the iron-barred fence of the gate like a winged guard. Behind the gate is the **Royal Residence (királyi rezidencia)**. The always changing Castle district with its many functional buildings is the separate empire of the **Palace**. Its story starts in the middle of the XIV. century, during the rule of the Hungarian kings who came from the Italian Anjou dynasty. Imagine when they first looked out this southern part of the hill, where the plateau narrows into an acute triangle perfect for building the royal residence. The wings which we can now walk around have not much in common with those of the medieval times. When observing the character of the façades and the main lines of the buildings it looks like a turn of the century construction, made by Hungarian craftsmen to fulfil the needs of Joseph Ferencz, the Austrian-Hungarian Emperor and King and his ever-increasing court. However, this picture, as we have already said, has changed much in the past 50 years. The **Royal Palace** suffered most from the damage inflicted during the Second World War. It was totally burnt out, practically all the pieces of furniture of the main rooms; the royal apartments, the ball room, the throne room were destroyed. The collapsed dome was

rebuilt in a simpler manner, and some of the north-west wings of the Palace had to be demolished because of their fragile state. Still preserved is its dignity, encapsulated in the magnificent collection of buildings which is the proud Castle of Buda. Its history started in the middle of the 1300s, when the first Anjou Hungarian king, Charles Robert decided to put his glamorous residence on the Castle Hill of Buda. The ground plan of this Roman-styled residential tower is shown by the different coloured stones built into the floor of the Upper Palace Court. The narrow windows of this tower's cellar can be seen at the bottom part of the terraced palace garden, which we will approach at the end of our walk in the Castle. The Castle was first significantly modified by Sigmound of Luxembourg, King of Hungary

The work of Schulek is a characteristic feature of Budapest's panorama

and Holy Roman Emperor in the first part of the XV. century. He extended the fortress, shifting the epicentre northwards. His great New Palace with its immense Hall of Knights, measured approximately 70◊20 metres, making Buda's Castle rank among the greatest in Europe. The size of the area covered by the Castle District surrounded by its fortified walls and bastions has changed to this day filling all the available space on the plateau. At the end of the XIX. century it was extended further spilling over the original triangle so that the walls here lean against the hillside of Krisztinaváros. Recently there have been numerous discoveries of Gothic sculpture which had probably

29

The statue of St. Stephen, the State Founder

alterations. He converted the whole palace into the renaissance style, finding the previous one not lavish enough for his taste. The green area, then a gorgeous garden, was created at this time on the eastern slope of the hill.
All that remains today of this past beauty is that which has been buried by the charitable earth. The destruction was brought on everything built until then by 150 years of Turkish invasion and occupation and the battles of the reconquest.

The Triumphal Arch

decorated the palace of Sigmound's son, Louis the Great. They were found by the fortunate László Zolnay in the seventies, creating a world sensation. A whole sculpture gallery of XIV. century Hungary! There is now an exhibition in the Historical Museum of Budapest, of all the sculpture fragments portraying bishops, lords and noble men.
King Matthias Corvinus, the greatest king since St. Stephen and possibly Béla IV., the renaissance emperor made the next major

The Royal Palace

The rebuilding started some decades later by the order of Queen Maria Theresa in the second half of the XVIII. century. There were some extensions carried out to the north, filling in the medieval moat. The wings form the shape of a "U" with the opening facing south. Finally, the last big building period began at the turn of the century. The south court was closed and the west wing was born. The arch with the turul bird, through which we finally enter, is also from this time. A magnificent stairway leads to the entrance of the Palace proper, where the steep east wall widens into the deep embrasure. Here stands the **Statue of Prince Eugene Savoy**, the leader of the military operations which led to the final withdrawal of the Turkish troops from Hungary. Here we can

The southern courtyard of the Palace

again enjoy a breathtaking panorama. Buda could be the city of nice panoramas, if there were such a title.

The double middle wing of the Palace, including the dome, is now occupied by the **National Gallery**. The National Gallery has the most complete collection of Hungarian paintings and sculpture. The old Hungarian collection displays the pictures painted on wood and wooden sculptures of the XIV–XV. century. Some of the most spectacular pieces of the collection include the richly gilded winged altars, once displayed in the throne room, which skilfully combine sculpture and painting. There are also many large paintings from Munkácsy Mihály and some picturesque panoramas painted by Csontváry Koszka Tivadar, who had a great influence on Modernism.

▷ *The Matthias Well, the jewel of the Palace courtyards*

The big Southern Round Bastion

Also to be found in the National Gallery is the entrance to the **Nádor-Crypt**, which was rebuilt a decade ago. The Habsburg noblemen and their families, who lived in Hungary at the beginning of the XIX. century, rest here in richly ornamented tombs.

In the other wings there are also museums. Their entrance is not here, at the extension of the stairway facing the Danube; we now have to walk through the narrow passage to the west side in order to reach them. A pretty garden and a preserved city of ruins displaying the finds of the excavations await the visitor.

The most interesting ornament in the square is the Matthias Well, which is perhaps the most beautiful fountain in Budapest. It pictures a hunting scene. It almost appears as though a forest stream fills the conch-shaped basin.

34

The bronze figures are the work of Alajos Stróbl, the great historical sculptor of the XIX. century. The Palace Square can be freely entered from the west and is bordered by an arch on the southern side. Behind the heavily encrypted lion-guarded gate the southern courtyard can be entered. Here the pavement patterns follow the outline of the medieval buildings of the ground plan of the **Stephen Tower**. To the right hand side is the large western wing where the **National Szécheny Library** welcomes visitors. This library contains the complete collection of national Hungarian books and other printed material. At the south end of the courtyard lies the entrance to the **Budapest History Museum**. The current exhibition halls were built using parts of the remains of Sigmound's and Louis the Great's castle, including, for example, the Great Hall of Knights. The restored Castle's chapel, once belonging to the Anjou castle is also part of the exhibition. Probably the richest display is the renaissance stone collection, which shows the lavishness of the Palace of Matthias Corvinus. As well as the permanent exhibitions, from time to time the palace houses temporary ones that attempt to display the 2000 years of Budapest's history.

Facing the door through which we entered the foyer of the museum, we step through another glass door which takes us to the top of a steep flight of steps. Five hundred years of history will gradually recede behind us as we descend. All that remains, all that was possible to recover and to reconstruct of the medieval royal castle and former fortress is here for our inspection. The small rectangular garden, the first we cross, is one of several such enclosures, which are located in the space between the walls separating the palace from the fortress and which served a defensive purpose no less important than the bastions or gate-towers. On our left, the grim stone wall of the XIV–XV. century cellar and the charming little courtyard

belonged to the first inhabitants of the fortress. Next a passageway. Now we are at the southern-most tip of the enclosed courtyards. This small enclosure once belonged to King Matthias's Palace. It has a **well** in the middle, embellished with coats of arms, and it is overlooked by the windows of the Great Hall of Knights, built in Gothic style. Under the Great Hall the aptly named **"cooling off chamber"(hűsölő)** was actually a cellar where the King's courtiers came to cool off out of the summer heat. On our left, a corridor decorated with lacy stone carvings, leads directly to the gates of the **Panting Gate (Lihegő Kapu)**. The name was given by the Turks, who found the ascent too steep, no doubt. The Gate gives access to the great **Southern Round Bastion (déli nagy rondella)** built by King Matthias. We descend from here towards the south-west end of the Castle, which is marked by a slim

The Mace Tower

The Elizabeth Bridge

tower, the **Mace Tower (Buzogánytorony)** built at the beginning of the XIV. century. Below this is the **Ferdinand Gate** through which we exit, leaving the Castle behind us.

Historical Buda bids us farewell with its well kept green slopes. We now enter the **Tabán** walking down a winding promenade. This area does not have many visible historical sights, compared with the Castle District. From the early Middle Ages until the XX. century this area was densely populated, mostly by Serbs. The name of the area comes from the Turks; Tabán, meaning slippers. The majority of the Serbs were involved with leather craft, making shoes and slippers, a profession highly valued by the Turkish officers and soldiers. The district was cleared of its dilapidated houses in the 1920s, many saw it as the sad passing of an era. The Tabán used to be the home of many inns, narrow winding badly lit streets, shut gates, cramped houses. Budapest mourned the loss of this romantic piece of history. A few of the nobler buildings were, however, preserved. One of these is the **Stag House (Szarvas-ház)** at the southern foot of Castle Hill. It used to be an inn for two or three hundred years. Nearer to the Danube, another Tabán landmark is the old church and its neighbour, the former **Parish House**. They were built between 1728 and 1736. These buildings also contain ruins of older buildings dating back to the time of Árpád. Evidence for this includes the Christ of Tabán to be found hiding in a small niche on the left-hand side of the Church. This stone figure was made in the XII. century.

Stepping out from the Church, we are greeted by the graceful **Elizabeth Cable Bridge**. It was named after the beautiful Queen of Joseph Ferenc, when it was built in 1903 (the statue of

Statue of St. Gellért

the ill-fated Queen stands in the park near the bridge on the Buda side). Elizabeth Bridge, destroyed in 1945, was known in its time for being the largest suspension bridge in the world. Its beauty and elegance were also without compare. Today's bridge was opened to the public in 1964. Its narrow, white silhouette strongly resembles its noble predecessor, looking like a giant seagull floating above the waves of the grey-blue waters.

Budapest could be described as the capital of Europe, not only for its many bridges, but also for its healing waters and thermal baths. Near the Elizabeth Bridge, at the base of the Gellért Hill lies a fault that supplies the hot springs for some of the many Baths, two of which are the **Rudas and Rácz Bath**. Among their wells the most interesting is the one named after Baba Gül (the patron of Buda in Turkish times), which is decorated with ornate cast-iron and lies at the foot of the cliff. The baths were first renovated during the Turkish occupation; if nothing else, the Muslims at least managed to

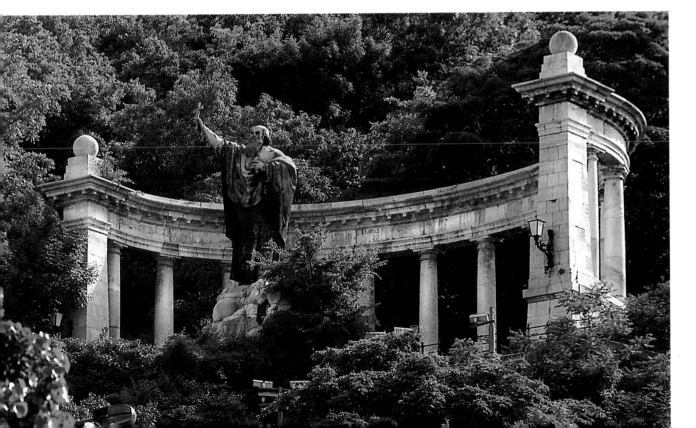

The Cliff Chapel of Gellért Hill

maintain the baths well. The Rudas Bath is separated from the Danube by the quay, but the hall beneath the Turkish dome, built by the two pashas of Buda, Ali and Sokoli Mustafa, can be best seen from the hillside.

On the northern side of Gellért Hill, in the Hadnagy utca (Lieutenant Street) lies Rácz Bath, named after the Serbs who once lived here. Its Turkish built, octagonal-shaped domed hall has welcomed visitors for more than four hundred years.

Now there is just one further stage in our tour; the Gellért Hill. Pretty white steps take us up first to the **bronze statue of St. Gellért** and then on to the top. The statue built in 1904 and designed by Gyula Jankovits stands almost twelve metres high and portrays the martyred bishop holding up the holy cross above the town. Bishop Gellért who was the priest of St. Stephen, Hungary's first king and also tutor to his son, Imre, became a victim of the pagan rebellions in 1046. He was captured by armed men and hurled down Kelen Hill in a barrel. To commemorate him the hill was renamed Gellért Hill.

At the very top of the hill is the **Citadel (Citadella)**. This fortress was built by the Austrian Emperor Joseph Franz (later crowned King of Hungary) in 1850 in order to control the rebellious Pest and Buda city. Today it is a peaceful tourist site with the military having departed around the turn of the century.

Also inhabiting the plateau at the top of this hill is a cluster of giant statues. The female figure holding up a palm leaf is fourteen metres high, and stands upon a twenty-six metre high pedestal. It was commissioned in 1947 in order to commemorate the Russian victory in the Second World War. The statue was the work of Zsigmond Stróbl Kisfaludi and was allowed to keep its place following the fall of communism in 1990, apart from the figure of the Russian soldier holding up the flag, the red star and the

Cyrillic inscriptions. Today, the monumental statue retains its commanding position over Budapest. Only its name has been changed from **Liberation** to **Freedom**.

We are now continuing our walk down the southern slope following the well-paved path offering many interesting views of the City. Our walk leads to another Danube bridge, the **Freedom Bridge (Szabadság-híd)**. We are going to learn more about this hundred year old artistic feat of iron-rigged engineering later, during our third walk. Before we get to the square by the foot of the hill, we stop at the **Cliff Chapel (Sziklakápolna)**, which was founded by the only Hungarian order of monks, the Pálosok (the Paulite Fathers), and built in

The Gellért Hotel and Baths

the natural caves to be found here. It was built and furnished as a church in 1926 following the style of the Lourdes caves of France.

At the base of the hill, near the entrance to the Chapel, the eye is drawn towards a picturesque group of buildings. These are the old **Gellért Hotel and Baths,** whose main attraction is their thermal waters. The healing waters, which have been enjoyed over the ages, were enclosed by these nice, new buildings and gardens in 1910. The Palace of Gellért, now a hotel, was finished in 1918. Its jacuzzi and "wavepool" are a famously elegant meeting place of Budapest, and of the guests of the Hungarian capital.

Second walk

HOUSES OF PARLIAMENT ◆ ST. STEPHEN BASILICA ◆ INNER CITY

The face of Buda is determined by the Middle Ages and its baroque style. The old Pest, the once-walled town to the left of the Danube, and its northern outskirts (the XVIII. century district called Lipótváros)

The Parliament's hall under the cupola...

... and its council chamber

were shaped by classicism and romanticism, the styles of the beginning of the XIX. century. If we were looking for traces of earlier times, we would only find them in the inner kernel of Pest, near the Vámház körút, Múzeum körút or at the southern part of Váci Street. It is the

structure of the streets and not that of the houses here, that recall the medieval times. The streets are narrow, winding, the rows of houses are short, there are no traces of the modern world's logic of disciplined straight lines. At the beginning of the XIX. century Pest expanded and improved its old structure. The city became fashionable. Many new multi-storey apartment buildings, town houses and offices appear, mirroring the prospering and developing economy, and in within a few years the walled Pest of single story buildings disappears without a trace. As the last town gates vanished (the Hatvani Gate standing at the crossing of Lajos Kossuth Street and Múzeum körút, was brought down in 1808), the city centre immediately swallowed the new

Parliament

district parallel to the Danube, the Lipótváros, which started from the Danube and continued up to the Great Boulevard. Here there is also an inner boundary, near Parliament. The town's development only expanded beyond the Lipótváros in the later part of the 1890s, towards the eve of XX. century, when the huge block of barracks, called the New Building, which stood obstructively on the present Freedom Square was cleared out of the way (we are going to arrive here soon, and will then discuss this square in greater detail). This was the time, when the houses, showing the architectural taste of the new era were born, the blooming neo-classicism, the eclecticism of the

turn of the century, formed a beautiful picture which is characteristic of the present city. These richly ornamented, elegant buildings line two wide, important roads. One is a ring, the other is a ray.

We start our tour with the **Országház**, the Hungarian **Houses of Parliament**. The foundations of which were laid in 1885, and a commemorative assembly was held here in 1886 to celebrate the 1000th year of the Hungarian state, but the huge building was only completed in 1904. The huge cupola with a height of ninety-six metres joins the wings of the former Lower and Upper Houses. Its total area is 17000 square metres with the corridors forming ten courtyards. Only the best craftsmen of the times were employed to work

The hall of the old Royal Mansion is decorated by a Lotz fresco

▷ *The pomp of the palace is also increased by the special stairway*

42

on every detail, for example on the fantastic lace-work of the cast iron gate, the chandeliers, the frescoes decorating the halls and the façade (especially the frescoes of the main stairway, painted by Károly Lotz which are breathtaking), the wooden pieces and the stained glass windows of Parliament. Within the fascinating main stairway, the ceiling of which is held up by columns of Swedish granite, stands a statue of the designer, Imre Steindl. He comfortably combined the many different styles to create one harmonious building. The giant cupola, decorated with a huge rose petal chandelier and with the statues of the Hungarian kings along the wall, the reception rooms and the council chambers, together are made unmistakably original by the elegant and antique interior. The characteristically large council rooms and reception halls are decorated with valuable Gobelins and oil paintings, among which the most valuable is the canvas of Munkácsy portraying the conquest of Hungary. This is, according to some, is the most beautiful Parliament in Europe.

In 1896 another noble edifice was built on the square, the former High Court of Justice. It was designed by Alajos Hauszmann. The rows of columns of the main façade support a timphanon. Its neo-renaissance hall is richly decorated by the allegoric frescoes of Károly Lotz. Today it houses the **Ethnographic Museum**. Among the buildings in Kossuth Square the oldest one is the **Ministry of Agriculture** built in 1880. Although built later, its style is closer to the classical style of the Middle Ages than to the fashionable styles of the end of that century. This is one of the few buildings, that kept its original purpose and function. The **gallery of its arcade** is worthy of attention, as portrayed along it are the country's greatest agriculturists (agriculture

◁ *16. Alkotmány Street*

The headquarters of the Hungarian National Bank

Centre of Finances and Banking House

being a major part of the Hungarian economy). At the northern end of the building, opposite main entrance of the Parliament, open the most elegant rows of apartments in the **Alkotmány (Constitution) Street**. It is worth walking these few hundred metres, in order to glimpse into the gates and stairways, and observe the various façades and ornaments. They were built in the years just before the turn of the century, at the time of the prosperous building era of burgeoning Budapest, and portrayed the grace and elegance of their times. Together they form an attraction worthy of our attention, conveying the values of the established metropolis, Budapest. Some of these buildings deserve a closer inspection; for example **No. 6**, which was built for the Forestry Commission. It was the headquarters of this long-standing professional and was decorated by many towers. **No. 12** is owned by the Unitary Church, **No. 16** houses the centre for journalist's pensions, and **No. 18** used to be the headquarters of a publishing house. Walking along, we arrive onto the main road once surrounding Pest, at the crossing of Váci körút and Bajcsy-Zsilinszy Street, where there are metropolitan apartments and buildings built at the same time. Near here for example, on the **corner of Béla Stollár Street**, stands the headquarters of an old daily paper, the Pesti Hírlap, which has been in print for more than 150 years. Now we are very close to the **Western Station's buildings** and its big hall. This site has dominated the area since the first Hungarian railway between Pest and Vác was opened in 1846. The iron-structured Great Hall (declared a historical monument), and its side wings were designed and manufactured by the Eiffel company of Paris. This is a remarkable piece of work, an unmatched engineering achievement worthy of the name of the French designer. After this little detour we get back to Bajcsy-Zsilinszky Street, and into the Alkotmány Street. Now we proceed along the street in the shade of the rows of houses until **Bank Street**. On its corner stands another substantial house, once the headquarters of a German paper of Pest, the **Neues Pester Journal** which ran for more than one hundred years.

Walking beside its façade, towards the inner core of the City, we get to the Palace of the **National Bank of Hungary** in Hold (Moon) Street. It was built according to the plans of Ignác Alpár in 1905, and was the last of the buildings erected at the site of the demolished

▷ *The building in Hold Street is a typical example of Hungarian Art Nouveau*

47

Typical majolica ornaments on the roof of 4. Hold Street

New Building. Its neighbour, **No. 4 Hold Street** is an internationally valued masterpiece designed by Ödön Lechner, the great Hungarian master of Art Nouveau, who bravely adopted the treasure motifs of national folklore. The façade, the doors, the windows, the roof structure and its ornaments, the stairways, even the design of the interior of what was once the **Post Office Savings Bank**, and is now a bank, present a detailed picture. It was built between 1899 and 1901.

Among the buildings in Hold Street, those are a few that resemble the old style of Lipótváros. We can spot them immediately as we walk along, towards the **Batthyány Memorial** with its eternal flame.

This gracefully simple construction is a very touching symbol. Its flame commemorates Lajos Batthyány, Prime Minister of the country's first independent government, who was executed by a firing squad on this Square in 1949.

This area once nestled in the dark shadow of the New Building's barracks. Until its destruction, mentioned earlier, this army building divided the district in two. There was the older inner part and also the newer quarter consisting of "only" hundred year old buildings. The results of the later period are the houses standing in Alkotmány Street, some of the ones in Bajcsy-Zsilinszky Street, but especially those standing in Báthory Street, the other street opening to the Memorial, plus those buildings standing now in **Szabadság Square** in the place of the ex-barracks. Most of them were built at the turn of the century, the New Building was brought down in 1898-99, and they, especially **Nos. 10., 11., 12., 13., 16.** surrounding the square in a polygon, represent the style of the modern city. The **Stock Exchange building**, today the headquarters of Hungarian

▷ *13. Szabadság Square*

48

Television, deserves some attention. It was built a bit later, and at the southern end of the Square. Next to this is the newest office building in Budapest, the huge modern Centre of Finances and Banking House.

Some of the houses in Hercegprímás Street, opposite Hold Street, again recall the classicist Budapest. Along St. Stephen Square and its neighbourhood the rows of the houses are about 150 years old. Among them, the Venetian-Gothic styled building built in 1855–57, to the plans of Franz Wieser, lies on the **corner of Hercegprímás Street and St. Stephen Square** and is probably the most interesting.

We will look at some of the houses and courtyards around here, but first we take a look at the largest cathedral in Budapest, the **St. Stephen Basilica (Szent István Bazilika)**. Its construction started in 1851 according to the plans of the architect, Joseph Hild, who also designed most of the houses in this district. After the maestro's death, the building was continued by Miklós Ybl. He successfully combined the classicist style of Hild with his own neo-renaissance ideas, which created a building typical of Budapest. There was one more famous architect, Joseph Kauser working on the great work. Under his supervision this grand Basilica was finally finished half

The St. Stephen Basilica

The main nave of the Basilica

▷ An altar in the Basilica with a fresco by Gyula
Benczúr

The József nádor Square

a century later in 1905. The ground plan of the Basilica is shaped like a Greek cross. The area is divided into nine barrel-vaulted parts, with a cupola in the middle. The statues in timphanon and in the tower niches, the statue ornaments of the cupola on the outside and of the shrine are all the works of Leó Fessler. The Church is rich in works of fine art. It is ornamented with the paintings and sculptures of the first Hungarian artists: Mór Than, Bertalan Székely, Gyula Benczúr, Károly Lotz, Alajos Stróbl, János Fadrusz, Pál Pátzay, Béni Ferenzy. The Szent Jobb (Saint Right), the mummified right hand of Saint Stephen, the most esteemed relic of the Christian Hungarian nationality, kept in a richly ornamental medieval glass case, is here. The wall behind the shrine of the Basilica (the parish church of Inner Lipótváros), backs on to Bajcsy-Zsilinszky Street, which used to be the main road to Vác. Also not far from here lies Andrássy Street, the prettiest avenue in Budapest (we will walk along it during our third walk). Now we turn into József Attila Street at the corner of Hercegprímás Street to get to the second street parallel to the latter. Here we can see some more of the one hundred and fifty year old houses from the period when Pest was rebuilt. In the spring of 1838, the time of the big flood when even the water was covered with blocks of ice, many hundreds of houses were destroyed. Following the catastrophe, Derra Naum, a rich Greek merchant, built his house right here on the corner. **No. 3 Október 6. Street** is a typical classical building. Its

faithfully represented stairway, the classical bars of the corridors and the pleasant enclosed courtyard with a garden are worth an extra look. The garden (and the well) were a typical addition to every house standing here. We can also take a look at others from the same period in the Október 6. Street. **No. 5** was built in 1820, **No. 7**, the Marcibányi-Palace, famous for its once lavish ballroom, was built in 1830–32., **No. 20** in 1818., **No. 22** in 1812.

Opening from this street, is a little oblong shaped park that has existed for more than two hundred and fifty years. Among the houses around the park are also some nice buildings connected to this first part of the city's restoration. **1. József nádor tér** preserves some classical features. Its arcade was renewed not

The arcaded rows of 1. József nádor Square

The Hungarian Academy of Sciences

long ago, and two faithful **replicas of the Minerva and Apollo statues**, masterpieces of art during the Reformation (the 1840s) and once standing in front of the entrance to a nearby bath, have been placed here. The house was designed by József Hild. The dwelling opposite us, built for Endre Kovács-Sebestyén, doctor to the Hungarian-friendly Habsburg Joseph, the Palatine of Hungary, has a more varying façade, built in the romantic style **(5–6. József nádor Square)**. The main focus of the square is not a building though. The **bronze statue of** the often mentioned **József nádor** is the oldest standing non-religious statue in Budapest. It was unveiled in 1869.

If we go towards the Danube from No. 1. leaving the statues of Apollo and Minerva, we get to a larger square. Before we have a look

around here, it's worth popping into the **chemist in the corner house**. We can still buy medicines in this shop, which has served the city since 1803. Every piece of furniture, the jars of medicine and the scales are like those in a museum.

On the southern part of Roosevelt Square are two luxurious hotels. They are the cherished work of Modernist architecture. However the square itself is not a "product" of today's town planning. Exactly the opposite, it is one of the oldest squares of Pest. At its birth it was surrounded by the docks for cargo ships, but by the beginning of the XIX. century it had expensive town houses all around it. Of those only one remains today, the large building on the corner of **Akadémia (Academy) Street**, built of course in the classical style of Pest, in 1835. Its ground floor was home for more than a hundred years to the most exclusive inn of the town, the **Hotel To The Archduke Stephen**. And since we are here, let's walk up to the next house in Alkotmány Street. The twin house to this is **No. 3**. József Hild which finished its design a year later, in 1836. Its courtyard, marble stairway and the well in the courtyard are worth mentioning separately. Together they make this building with its decoration one of the masterpieces of Hungarian neo-classical architecture.

The most beautiful building on Roosevelt Square is the headquarters of the **Hungarian National Academy of Sciences (Magyar Tudományos Akadémia)**. It was built according to the award-winning plans submitted by the Prussian Frigyes Stüler, between 1862 and 1865. The character of its neo-renaissance façade is quite different from the previously discussed buildings. These peculiar architectural features are probably the most visible in the hall and its ornamental stairway.

This is an attractive building in every detail. The frescos are painted by Károly Lotz. There is the gallery of the Academy on the third floor, which is especially rich in the works of classical Hungarian artists.

On the Square, near the Academy is the **bronze statue of Count István Szécheny**. It was unveiled in 1880. The "Greatest Hungarian" stands on a granite post facing towards his greatest achievement, the Chain Bridge. Some ten metres away is a living historical object; the **oldest tree of the Capital**, an old Acacia, planted in the 1840s. Its waist is supported by beams, its branches are more dry, than green. Its eternal life has been ensured, should its demise become imminent; cuttings have been taken from the original and replanted (some are now ten years old) in order to take the place of their parent, even at a young age, when the

The Gresham House representing the Art Nouveau

Hotels on the Promenade of the Danube

Life on the Danube bank

time comes to be one of the oldest trees in Budapest.

Standing on the Square, opposite the Bridge, is a derelict building in art nouveau style, the **Gresham House**. Walking in its courtyards and stairways, we can get an impression of how lavish this building must have been during its heyday. Hopefully it will be again after its restoration. It was built in 1907 as the headquarters of the Gresham Insurance Company.

There are two more statues in the park. One is of **Ferenc Deák**, the main figure in the Great Compromise of 1867, who entered Hungarian history as the wise man of the

Nation. The other one is the bronze figure of **József Eötvös**, who was the great reformer of Hungarian education. This statue stands in front of the **Hotel Atrium** on the Square named after him. It is worth popping into the hall of the hotel; an elegant, modern atrium greets us, a green island closed behind glass walls. This is a recreation of the old gardens in the courtyards of Lipótváros. Going around the statue to the right, we take a walk by the main façade of the hotel looking at the river, on the famous **Promenade of the Danube (Dunakorzó)** which offer excellent attractions. Its predecessor, the row of trees planted at the southern end, started its career more than two hundred years ago, at the raft by the parish church of the centre. The later version, improved with the additions of benches and pretty attractive street

The Redoute

lights, was built about a hundred years ago, for the Millennium, when walking along there became fashionable. The bourgeois of the city walked there and not only to Váci Street, the old promenade, on warm summer nights and on Bank holiday afternoons to spend their time admiring the city and its inhabitants.

In the middle of the promenade stands the first elegant music hall of Pest, the **Vígadó (Redoute)**, built as a dance and concert hall in 1859–64, and including a restaurant, clubs and a pool room. This is the most outstanding piece of Hungarian romanticism, built by Frigyes Feszl. Its frescos and ornamental statues celebrate the work of the best artists of that time; Károly Lotz and Mór Than. Its richly proportioned façade, decorated by symbolic and historical statues, is a charming addition to the promenades.

Going past the Vigadó, along Vigadó Street,

we enter some of the oldest parts of Pest.
Vörösmarty Square is basically the hub of this
old town. In the middle stands the Carrara
marble statue of the poet (Mihály Vörösmarty)
writing "Proclamation"; whom the Square is
named after. The outline of the former gate,
Váci kapu, named after the town of Vác, can be
seen here, in the patterns of the pavement.
Vörösmarty Square joins Váci Street to the
promenade, and so it is also a popular scene for
couples walking. Its most remarkable building
is the Gerbeaud House with its famous confec-
tionery. Its founder came from Switzerland
more than a hundred years ago. The tasty
pastries and sweets are still made to his recipes,
and the interior also recalls old times.
In front of us lies the **Váci Street**, the pulsing,
busy centre of Pest, and the City, where the

Vörösmarty Square

▷ *Váci Street*

58

Ornate façade on the Szervita Square

banks and elegant fashion shops can be found, jostling for position, next to each other. Old houses recalling the past hardly exist here any more. One that does however is the house standing on the corner of Kristóf Square opening on the left, not far after the gate outline **(No. 4 Váci Street)**. Another is **No. 9, Váci Street** with its stairway of classical statues and its corridor with Doric columns. Both houses were built in 1840. The buildings under **Nos. 10** and **21** are older still. They were built in 1800 and 1805 respectively.

This is all there is left from the five hundred year old street. Everything else has been built around the turn of the century or later, and is still developing.

We have now arrived at **Szervita Square**, named after the Servita order, in the centre. Their **church**, dominating the Square, was built in 1725–32 whilst its tower was built 1871. The inside is baroque, the outside is eclectic, because of its many restorations. The masterpieces of the XVIII. century richly ornament the walls and altars.

The neighbour to the holy house is the **Town Hall (Központi Városháza)**. This is one of the few baroque buildings in Pest. It was built as a Monarchy Veterans hospital between 1724 and 1774 to the plans of the Italian Fortunato de Prati. It remained a hospital until the end of the XIX. century, when it was modified to be used as the office of administration of Budapest. There is not much left from the old times since the new owners moved in except the vaulted corridors, window settings, closed courtyards, its main gate and the three-figured Atlas composition above it.

7. Városház utca (Town Hall Street), the multi-courtyarded **County Hall (Vármegyeháza)** is a very strange looking building. The office of administration of Pest County once used to work here from the beginning of the XIX. century. Here were the rooms of its ornamental council hall and its less attractive prison. This was the well guarded island of the county in the metropolis. Its nicest part is the arcaded classical front courtyard with columns, rebuilt in 1838–41, and the columned gateway leading there. It is worth walking through the courtyards for a museum of the old or unwanted statues of the city is organised here. The beautiful, graceful Hebe by József Huber (who also carved the earlier mentioned Apollo and Minerva statues) can be found here along with some works of another gifted sculptor of

The Kossuth Lajos Street

the Reformation, Lőrinc Dunaiszky. In addition there are some sculptures from wells of courtyards that have disappeared, and the neo-Gothic well head from the demolished 12. Dorottya Street.

Crossing the courtyards of the County Hall, turning to right on Semmelweis Street, we get to the main road of medieval Pest. In modern times it was widened and renamed as **Kossuth Lajos Street**. As most of its buildings were built around the turn of the century, there is only one old building left, the **Franciscan church** (built in 1727–1743) near to Elizabeth Bridge, whose present shape was built in 1861. In the middle of its façade are the baroque sculptures of St.

Peter, St. Francis and St. Anthony. Above the gate are Maria with Jesus and the angels. Its interior is also mainly baroque, the altars and the organ loft unmistakably show signs of this style.

Getting to know some of the churches in Budapest, and in Hungary, you may ask why the majority of them are baroque. The explanation is simple, but not very cheerful. Between 1541 and 1686, under the Turkish invasion, practically everything was destroyed of the flourishing medieval Hungary. Everything had to be rebuilt from its foundations in the XVIII. century, and at that time the baroque style was already dictating architectural taste in Europe, and also in the capital, Budapest. Here, around the Elizabeth Bridge the medieval Pest was built. The seedlings of the right hand town started to grow here, looking for support to the embrace of the Roman walls. These walls, excavated after the turn of the century and transformed into a museum, are still clearly visible. This was the Roman fortress, already on the "land of the barbarians", as Rome called the area on this side of the Danube. In 294 AD, by the order of Caesar Diocletianus, a towered castle was built on the former site. There are documents proving that the first Hungarians coming with these conquerors built their parish church, their houses and built streets in the area between the long empty **Roman castrum** and the Danube. The descendant of this Church still stands here today. It has been rebuilt twice from ruins. The Roman styled version was burnt down during the Tartars' ravages in the XII. century. It was again destroyed during the Turk invasion and only the bare walls remain. The **Inner City Parish Church (Belvárosi Plébániatemplom)** was of course rebuilt in baroque style to a high standard according to the plans of György Paur, between 1725 and

◁ The Inner City Parish Church with the ruins of the Castrum

The Orthodox Serbian Church

1739. The inside of the Church is a rich museum of religious artefacts, tracing eight centuries of time. There is a stone collection in the crypt with some renaissance marble fragments, showing that the Church was probably rebuilt during the time of King Matthias. The majolica stone altar by Zsolnay has suffered irreparable damage in the second World War and had to be replaced, allowing in the modern looking altar by Pál C. Molnár in its place. It covers a complete cross-section of tastes and ages, a renaissance holy-water font (southern side entrance), pre-romantic pulpit (1808.), renaissance niches (side chapel, 1507.), baroque side altars from the 1700s, nineteen sedilas (recessed benches) from the XV. century, and one Turkish praying niche (mihrab) by the end of the sedilas, to the right. There are many gravestones, one to look at is the one standing to the left hand side of the first side chapel. This, made from white marble in 1828, commemorates István Kultsár, the editor, and was erected by his widow. It was carved by the best sculptor of that time, István Ferenczy. Kultsár was the first man in Hungarian history, who had a main career in literature, and who lived comfortably by it. In those times, in the first quarter of the 1800s, the middle classes were already wealthy enough, that many of them could afford to choose to be intellectuals. To the north from the Inner City Parish Church, beyond the university building, is the only **baroque civilian house (barokk polgárház)**, which survived the earlier destruction and times of restoration. This elegant town house was generally kept as an inn. The Hundred Year

The Viaduct tram

The Margaret Bridge from the Pest side

Old (Százéves) Inn has been run in this building since 1831. It was designed by András Mayer-hoffer, and was ready in 1755 **(1. Galamb utca, 2. Piarista utca)**.

The southern end of the Promenade of the Danube is at the end of this row of houses. There is a little square bulging out on the river bank on which stands the **bronze statue of** Hungary's greatest national poet, **Sándor Petőfi**, erected through donations in 1882. Facing the Statue, the **church** with the single tower once belonged to the city's Greek community **(2. Petőfi Sándor tér)**. This community, numbering some hundred wealthy families, came in the XVIII. century along the trade routes, and opened shops, bought citizenship and after some time became members of the elite, some achieving the status of counts and even barons. The centre of their colony, along Galamb Street, became the victim of town planning around the millennium, including the huge buildings with many courtyards behind the Church. Still visible, outside the back wall of the Church, are the strangely written grave stones set into the wall of their long dead nobles, the Panajots, Sacelláry, the Sinas, the Nakos, the Naums, the Bekells. The Church itself was built to the plans of József Jung between 1791 and 1801. Its red marble main gate and the towers (the original southern tower was destroyed in the war) are the result of a reconstruction in 1874. These plans were made by Miklós Ybl, in a braided style mixed with some baroque and classicism. The superb iconostasis and interior are the work of Miklós, dating from 1794–1799.

Let's walk back to the Promenade. We recommend a ride on the tram which is hundred years old. The **viaduct tram** is very special as it goes along above the quay offering a spectacular panoramic ride. To the right-hand side is the Promenade, to the left is Buda with all its sights. We are going to pass Lajos Kossuth Square, where we have already been, when we started our walk at the Parliament. We are going to the last stop, to the Pest end of **Margaret Bridge (Margit híd).**

This was the second permanent bridge over the Danube. The Great Boulevard (Nagykörút), the second ring, leads here. We can see the slowly arching row of houses to the right. Margaret Bridge is also arched, in order to get near to **Margaret Island (Szent Margit szigete)** as well as to join the two parts. Until then the island could only be reached by boat. Its construction began in 1872, the wing to the island being finished in 1900. It was built according to the plans of Guoin Ernest, a French engineer under the supervision of the Construction des Battignoles in Paris. The street-lights resemble the lights of the Place de la Concorde in Paris, although the carved sections were made in the craft shop of Thabard. This is a piece of Paris in Budapest, in the same way that the area around the Western Station is a piece of London. By the time the Bridge was opened to the public in 1876, Budapest was no longer Pest and Buda (and Óbuda), it was one town with a single administration. The change in status led to speedy alterations, of which we have already talked. We will go into more detail about these changes during our third walk, but before that we must take a big step back in time. Walking along the wing leading to the island we find ourselves in the Middle Ages. This land was civilised in the XII. century by the Order of Johannite fighting for Christianity, which was brought to Hungary, together with other Orders by St. Stephen. He was the Hungarian king, crowned in the year 1000 by the then Pope, Sylvester, and in doing this he became registered on the list of Christian kings, and Hungary on the list of European countries. The four turreted castle of the Johannites' stood near the southern end of the island. The guest house of the Crusaders also used to stand here, a place where they could rest during their expeditions. At the same time the first of the Orders moved to the Island of Hare (this was the first known name of the Island). From the second half of the XIII. century, the Franciscans, the Premonstratensians, later the Augustines and the Dominicans had their monasteries here. During this time the Island kept its fortressed style. This is the time of legendary history, the bitter-sweet story of a princess. Béla VI. promises to the Lord, that if the Tartars leave the country, he will give his only daughter to an order and build its convent, where the beautiful woman could begin her saintly life.

The cloisters, convents and monasteries controlled the area for a long time, until the end of the XVIII. century, when the Habsburg Regents chose it as the summer place of the Hungarian Palatines. For a while, its name became Palatinus, however, the name Margaret Island which came from the XIV. century was retained as its official name. It was designated a public garden, and from this time onwards the public were freely allowed to use it (before that it could only be visited with an entrance ticket). There is another important event from this period; the thermal water, already richly found everywhere under Budapest was also discovered here in 1866 using a process of deep-boring by Vilmos Zsigmondy, the famous Hungarian hydro-engineer. This made the Island's climatic healing powers even more widely accepted.

Today this Island is one of the city's favourite places for excursions. There are sport courts,

The Water Tower on Margaret Island

ancient gardens, swimming pools, hotels, restaurants, thermal water pools, an open air theatre, and other enjoyments to await the visitor on this one hundred hectare, two and a half kilometres long and 500 metre wide paradise in the heart of the City. Its lush greenery is reflected in the legendary romantic story of St. Margit, and the Orders that once lived here, the picturesque ruins of the convents and its reconstructed churches.

The **Church and Convent of the Dominican nuns** is single-naved, its chancel and oratory being last reconstructed in the XV. century. The windows of the sacristy belong to the Romanesque period. The square-shaped two-

There is thermal water in the pools of the rock garden on the Island

storey high **Convent** stands on the southern side with a cloister and a well-house. **The funerary Chapel of St. Margaret** is situated on the right-hand side of the façade. Excavations started in 1838 and at present, only its preservation is a problem. The reconstruction of the **Premonstratensian Church of St. Michael** was only carried out recently. The medieval **Chapel** near it was found as recently as 1923. The **Franciscan Church** was consecrated in 1272. The extant wall and the remains of the tower are part of the northern façade. Of the newer buildings on the Island, the **Grand Hotel** was opened in 1873, and has been the centre of tourism for 125 years. Today it is the Ramada Grand Hotel. The **Casino**, designed by Miklós Ibl around 1860, is an elegant place for entertainment at the southern end of the Island. Situated near the northern end, the replica of the musical fountain was built in 1936. The **Bodor Well**, named after the Transylvanian craftsmen used to play melodies every hour with the golden Nepumuk turning on the top, and was powered by water. The original, in Transylvania, built in 1820, has been long since destroyed. This replica was damaged during the war and was renovated in the 1980s, although its clockwork motion and musical system could not be repaired.

NATIONAL MUSEUM ♦ OPERA HOUSE ♦ HEROES' SQUARE

The tightly walled medieval Pest, used to have three main roads which approached four gates. The gates were surrounded by houses that sprang up from the earliest times, gradually populating larger and larger areas expanding beyond the town walls as well as within. The remains of the walls demolished in the XVIII. century can still be seen in the courtyards of nearly all of the houses that are along the Danube side of the **Múzeum körút (Museum Boulevard)**, for example **Nos. 21, 23–25, 27, 29, 33, 41**. The reason that sections of the walls still remain is that they were an integral part of the walls of the houses that were built before the XVIII. century. These houses were built both to the inside and outside of the walls. These houses later give way to larger, more elegant, town-houses that were built during the first rebuilding period at the beginning of the XIX. century.

A beautiful example of these newer houses is the **Unger House (No. 7 Múzeum körút)**, which stands near the site of the old Hatvani Gate. The proprietor of this house originally owned a famous blacksmiths just inside the gate; due to its location he prospered allowing him to have the Unger House built. It was designed in 1852 by the well-known architect, Miklós Ybl, in the romantic style. Its balcony, decorated with griffins, and its arcaded courtyard, make this property a warm reminder of romantic architecture in Pest. The courtyard has a public thoroughfare running through it.

The floor is paved with oak blocks, half of which are still the originals from the middle of the XIX. century. In those days oak paving was applied not only to courtyards, but also to roads and pavements in order to reduce dust. This surprisingly hard-wearing surface also quietened the sound of horses' hooves and rolling carriage wheels. As we walk through the thoroughfare and step out of the Gate to **Magyar Street**, we find ourselves in a typical medieval street of Pest; the street curves follow the former wall and it is as narrow as it can be. We start off towards the park, on the left, which is the only reasonable sized park in the Inner City. This is the beautiful **Károlyi-kert (Charles Park)**. Not always a public garden, it belonged to the residential building to the west, which now houses the **Petőfi Literary Museum (Petőfi Irodalmi Múzeum)**, our next destination **(16. Károlyi Mihály Street)**. The Károlyi Mansion has stood here since the middle of the XVIII. century. Its present classical character was created in the 1830s. The exceptionally spacious gateway, its Doric row of columns and the gilded stucco-worked ceremonial hall with a white marble stove, all praise the ostentatious taste of its past owners.

We now start walking to the left, towards Lajos Kossuth Street. Here there is an exceptional building lifting its cupola to the skies; the **Library of the University**, on the corner of Reáltanoda Street **(10. Károlyi Mihály Street)**. This neo-renaissance building with a sgrafitto

decorated façade was built in the middle of the 1870s. The great reading room is decorated with the frescos of Károly Lotz.

Further along, there is an old restaurant, called **Kárpátia**, near to the Ferenciek tere (Square of the Franciscans), where the Franciscan Church that we visited on our earlier walks stands. This restaurant has been here since the middle of the 1870s (when the building was built in place of the Franciscan Monastery), and was very popular among the food-loving citizens of the Capital with its draught beer and delicious luncheons. Its present elegant look was created

◁ *21. Múzeum Boulevard*

The Károlyi Garden

during the years of the former golden age of hospitality in Pest in the twenties, when the appropriate surroundings were considered to be of great importance to the guests.

Walking in the other direction away from the Károlyi Mansion, we now take a look at two churches in the southern part of the ancient Inner City. Opposite the Mansion, behind the central building of the Eötvös Lóránt University, stands the **University Church** and the headquarters of the **Academy of Theology** in **Papnövelde Street**. The Church belongs to the Paulite Fathers, who started construction in

71

1722. It took exactly fifty years to finish and the west tower was completed in 1771. This Church, consecrated in 1776 is probably the pearl of the baroque in Budapest, filled with interior ornaments and relics also representing the style. The pulpit is an outstanding example of baroque art in Hungary. The ornaments on the pews and on the choir's door and the entrance gate are the skilful work of the Paulite Father Felix. The main altar, dated from 1746 has a richly varying mixture of styles.

The **three-storey Seminary (7. Papnövelde Street)**, today the Academy of Theology was built as the **Cloister** to the Paulite Fathers in the 1770s. It was renovated in the neo-renaissance

◁ *The building of the University Library*

The Central Market Hall

style away from the previous one of the baroque. This is an exceptionally beautiful place representing the interior decorative style of that era with its fresco by Károly Lotz; a two-storey reading-room in the library (with richly carved bookshelves, a baroque railed gallery and a spiral staircase), and the fresco by Pietro Rivetti on the ceiling, dated to 1803. Papnövelde Street opens into Veres Pálné Street. We proceed to the left, southwards, leaving behind the busy streets of the Inner City, until we reach **Szerb Street** on the next corner. Its main attraction is the **Orthodox Serbian Church**, which was built in 1695 by the Serbs who fled the Turks and found a home in Pest, and other villages along the Danube **(4. Szerb Street)**. While the basic exterior was created in 1733, the iconostasis was built in 1857. The garden behind, with its tombstones (much older than the ones in Galamb Street), and ancient trees, is a miniature enclave guarding the memory of the old community. The braided styled garden-gate with the sacred niche portraying St. George fighting with the dragon is special. The ruins in the garden were the remains of another, third, Serbian church in Budapest, which once served the orthodox community of the Tabán. It was pulled down after World War II.

The garden's other entrance, usually shut, opens to the courtyard of 66. Váci Street, which was built in 1874 as a community hall for the Serbian parish. Standing next to it (No. 62–64) is the **New Town Hall**, which has one of the most beautiful ceremonial halls in the Capital (and of course, the frescos of Lotz are present here). This is the hall where town representatives hold their meetings. This neo-renaissance building was designed by Imre Steindl, the architect of the Parliament, and was finished in 1875, when some of the Capital's offices moved in. Its main feature is its ornamental iron-structured main staircase, which has five branches going off it.

We return to the Danube at the southern end of Váci Street. In front of us there is the large neo-renaissance building, the **Fővámház (the main custom-house)**, built between 1871 and 1874 under the supervision of Miklós Ybl. Today it houses the **University of Economics in Budapest (Budapesti Közgazdaság Tudományi**

Its goods themselves are also attractions

The Freedom Bridge

▷ *The coat of arms on the pillar of the Freedom Bridge*

The National Museum

Egyetem). Next to it is the elegant **Central Market Hall (Központi Vásárcsarnok)**, the largest enclosed market in Budapest, built in 1896 and recently renovated. This multi-storey building packed with produce is itself an attraction. It has been visited by such guests to the capital as Queen Elizabeth and Chancellor Kohl.

To the right is the **Szabadság híd (Freedom Bridge)**, which we passed by during our first walk. This was the third bridge built, in 1896, and was at that time named after the ruler of the Austro-Hungarian Empire, Franz Joseph. It was the longest Gerber-structured bridge in the world, which means that the pieces going towards the middle of the Danube from the two pillars are held together by an independent central third party. This simple but grand idea was first used "to full scale" by a Hungarian engineer, János Feketeházy, when building the shortest Danube bridge.

The inner ring, following the line of the former town wall reaches the river by this bridge. This separates the outskirts from the former Pest. The first outskirts to be built were the Ferenc and József, and higher up the Teréz and Erzsébet Towns. We reach the József Town (Józsefváros) at Kálvin tér (Kálvin Square), with the Múzeum körút (Museum Boulevard) as its boundary. The newer town houses are on the even-numbered side, built during the years of prosperity in the first part of the XIX. century. Protruding from them is the **National Museum (Nemzeti Múzeum)**, with its garden packed with statues, and its robust stairway with columns crowned by a timphanon. It was designed by Mihály Pollack, one of the greatest architects of the XIX. century, between 1837 and 1847. The frame of the main entrance follows the pattern of the famous Erechteion in Athens. The statues on the timphanon are carved by Raffaello Monti. The ornaments of the interior are by Károly Lotz and Mór Than. The basis of the collection was from the private collection of Count István Szécheny, which he donated to the Nation in 1802. There are more than one million works of art, including objects connected with Hungary's history, from before its formation, until the present day. The permanent exhibition, opened in 1996 for the Millecenntenary of the Hungarian state, has on display many beautiful and important artefacts, painting an interesting picture of the past centuries. There is another permanent exhibition, displaying the **Hungarian Crown Jewels**. These early medieval treasures are especially valuable due to their historical value. There is the golden Crown of St. Stephen decorated with pearls, precious stones and enamelled vignettes together with the thousand year-old Coronation robe embroidered with

The Hall of the Museum of Industrial Arts

Ten minutes from the National Museum, on the Üllői road stands the Museum of Industrial Arts, the work of Ödön Lechner. This is probably the most beautiful building of Hungarian Art Nouveau. Its construction was finished in 1896, in the year of the Millennium.

golden thread, which is a rarity in the world, the rock-crystal sceptre; the man-sized sword with its ornate scabbard, all of which are the holy symbols of the Hungarian state. Coronation became a valid constitutional act a thousand years ago, and one of its requirements was that the person elevated to the throne touched these objects.

The Hungarian National Museum stands on the site of Józsefváros (József Town). Around it stand the town-houses of the aristocrats, in the **Magnate's Quarter (Mágnásnegyed)**.

It became fashionable soon after the opening of the National Collection to have a winter residence in the Capital in this area. Behind the Museum is the **Károlyi Palota (Károlyi**

3. Pollack Mihály Square

▷ *The Gschwindt House on the corner of Puskin and Bródy Street*

Mansion), the neo-renaissance work of Miklós Ybl built in 1863–65 **(3. Mihály Pollack Square)**. The **residence of the Eszterházy Dukes (8. Mihály Pollack Square)** was built in 1865, to the plans of Alajos Baumgarten in eclectical style. Its beautiful French cast-iron gate and fence (recently renovated), marks the boundary of the property. There is no garden any more, the glass-walled office building of Hungarian Radio now occupies its place. **No. 10 Pollack Mihály Square** used to belong to the **family of the Festetich Dukes.**

It was built under the supervision of Miklós Ybl in 1862, also in neo-renaissance style. Another **mansion belonging to Count Károlyis in Múzeum Street (No. 17)** was built in 1881 by the order of Count István to the plans of Ferdinánd Fellner and Hermann Helmer, who also designed many of the theatres in Pest. There is now an engineering library open to the public in the neo-baroque building. Its lavish stairway is worth taking a look at. There is another elegant building on the corner of **Ötpacsirta (Five Skylark) Street**, the **mansion of the Almássy Counts**. At the end of Ötpacsirta Street stands the most intact mansion of the district, the public library of the Capital, built in 1887 under the instructions of **Baron Wenckheim** to the plans of Artur Meinig in neo-baroque and rococo style. The rococo ornaments, stuccoes of the rooms (the present reading rooms), the furniture, the wooden casing and the chandeliers all create a wonderful overall effect. On the other side of Múzeum körút, there are also similar elegant town-houses. The building with a varying façade on the **corner of Sándor Bródy Street and Puskin Street** was designed for the baron **Gschwindt** family a little later, just after the turn of the XX. century. **No. 8 Sándor Bródy Street**, the **old Council Chamber**, was built in 1865–66 under the supervision of

◁ *The Adam House*

The balcony of the Adam House is ornamented with a Lotz fresco

József Diescher. This is where the **Members of Parliament of the Lower House** used to sit before the present Parliament was built. **No. 4** is the **Adam House**, an example of a citizen's house with Lotz frescos on its first floor loggia and ornamental sgrafitto in its gateway. The façade was built from ragged stone. This neo-renaissance building was the work of Antal Weber, who finished it for its commissioner, Károly Ádám, a fashionable doctor, in 1876.

Now we walk back to Kálvin Square, and from here we can travel by either underground or foot, towards the north along the Múzeum

körút. Going past the **old building of the University**, which was built in 1890, and past the crossing of Rákóczi Street, we arrive at the beginning of **Dohány Street (Tobacco Street)**, to found here stretching its dual domed head of radiant colours is the biggest **Synagogue** of Europe. It has more than three thousand seats in it. It was built according to the plans of Lajos Förster, the Viennese architect, with the help of the Hungarian maestro Frigyes Feszl, in 1854–59. Its style can be described as romanticism, mixed with Byzantine-Moor elements, giving this huge, ceramic decorated building a particular oriental taste and atmosphere.

There is the arcaded church and war memorial to the Jewish martyrs along the Dohány Street side, which was built in the XX. century, between 1929 and 1931. Also here stands the **memorial of the Hungarian Jewish martyrs** (made by Imre Varga in 1991). This metal composition, forming a willow tree, preserves the names of the citizens of Budapest (they are inscribed in its lines), who had been killed during the months of the holocaust. There is the **Hungarian Jewish Museum** in the building, which contains many articles of value and the documents of the life of the Jews in both the capital and the rest of Hungary.

We reach Deák Square along Károly körút, which is a continuation of Múzeum körút, and continue on until **Andrássy Street**. During the second period of the large scale restoration of Pest-Buda, those aspiring metropolitan ambitions started the grand task here by slicing into the mass of disorganised houses in the outskirts by these two major roads. The town elders had already decided in the 1870s to build and open the exceptionally wide avenue stretching from the border of the town to the City Park and the second boulevard (the Great Boulevard

◁ *The great Synagogue*

The memorial of the Hungarian Jewish Martyrs

– Nagykörút). With the opening of the latter the town exceeded its old boundaries, swallowing the new areas into the radius of renewal, and totally filling all the available space up to the boulevard by the turn of the XX. century. Building around the avenue of Pest, the Andrássy Street, followed three different patterns. The section between the Basilica and the Nagykörút, until Oktogon, is lined with a kilometre of elegant apartment buildings. After Oktogon, and until the next square, Kodály körönd, the houses stand a little further back, leaving some space for our great grandfathers who wanted to ride towards the Park. Beyond this Square, with its four historical statues and huge one hundred and fifty year old sycamore maples, the scene changes again. Villas and mansions are here; elegant houses with varying façades and turrets; the homes of the aristocrats and upper-middle classes. Similar houses to these can also be found in the streets opening on to Andrássy Street and beyond, especially on its right-hand side, where a villa quarter developed at the same time as the boulevard was built.

The Andrássy Street shows a unique architectural unity, even with these three divisions, because it didn't take more then ten years to complete the boulevard. Building began in 1872, and by 1884 there was only one empty space left along it, which was filled a year later.

Around the 1880s, another series of constructions begins as grand as the ones previously mentioned. Following a long dried-out river, long rows of elegant apartment buildings were built along the **Great Boulevard (Nagykörút)**, and by the year of the millennium, nearly every single area was occupied, including this one. Analysing these events, we can say that it is indeed very rare in Europe for the main face of a metropolis to develop in just twenty years. This stormy period of renewal and growth in Budapest created a uniquely homogeneous city.

We can find interesting buildings along the inner part of Andrássy Street as well as on the Nagykörút, and along the rows of apartments leading to the Park. In the gateway and stairway of **No. 3 Andrássy Street**, the Saxlehner House,

The Andrássy Street with the Millenary Monument in its axis

we can enjoy the Lotz frescos, and in **No. 2** the chandeliers in the hall are exceptionally beautiful. At **No. 9**, the gate decorated with atlases is also worthy of a mention. The two Flora-statues at the gate of **No. 23** are the work of the famous Hungarian sculptor, Alajos Stróbl. Its neighbour, the **Drechsler-Mansion (No. 25)** is one of the nicest eclectic-style buildings in Budapest designed by Ödön Lechner and Gyula Pártos.

Naturally, there are architectural masterpieces on the even-numbered side of the boulevard, for example **Nos. 8, 10, 12, 20 and 28**. The most valuable building, the **Hungarian State Opera House** also ornaments this side **(No. 22)**, and was commissioned by Miklós Ybl between

The Opera House

1875 and 1884 using every invention of those times in order to make it more lavish. The Opera House is a neo-renaissance building with baroque elements. The ornaments of the façade, enriched by statues, are repeated on the stairway, in the auditorium, in the assembly hall and on the royal balcony. The noble work of the finest artists, Mór Than, Árpád Feszty, Károly Lotz contribute to the elevated atmosphere of this place.

As we reach the boulevard, we commence another walk. We are going to walk along a one kilometre stretch on the right of the longest and, probably, the busiest road in Pest, the

The auditorium of the Opera House ...

... and its stairway

Teréz and Erzsébet körút (Theresa and Elizabeth Boulevards). We can take a look at the long rows of the interesting, varying façades, the ornamented roofs of the buildings, their turrets, statues and stucco variations, as if we were looking at the pages of a living town-planning album.

We walk along the *"young, charming Pest"*, as the enthusiastic inhabitants of the reborn modern city called it a hundred years ago. We can see here together all the features of Budapest that gain it the rank of metropolis. And to make the illusion perfect, lets step into one of the buildings. **No. 11. Erzsébet körút** is the famous **New York Palace (New York palota)**, ornamented with white laced turrets, now a little run down and reinforced with wooden supports. It was inaugurated in 1895

The National Ballet Institute

by the owner, an international insurance company and was designed by Alajos Hauszmann. It gives home to probably the only cafeteria, working in its original pomp, of which there used to be hundreds and hundreds at the turn of the XX. century.

We wouldn't now think when looking at the broken down state of the building, of what beauty lies hidden behind the grey, dilapidated old walls. The frescos of the former New York, now Hungária Cafeteria were painted by Gusztáv Magyar-Mannheimer, and by Károly Lotz, of course. Its marbled, silver mirrored, precious metal ornamented multi-leveled interior was created by the best Hungarian craftsmen. Its light hasn't faded during the last hundred years, and in fact has been brightened a little, with the fact that the greats of Hungarian literature, like Ferenc Molnár, the world famous playwright and his company, once sat at the tables of its lower part, the so called "deep water".

Getting back to Andrássy Street, we continue our journey on its grass-stripped pavement, then on its cobbles, toward the nicest park of the city, the City Park (Városliget). We will have the opportunity to look at some more pretty buildings, three of them are the **old Music Academy** under **No. 67, No. 69**, the building of the **old Art Gallery**, and **No. 71**, the corner building of the **College of Hungarian Fine Arts**. On the other side of the street stands one of the largest and most beautiful buildings, the **House of the Pallavicini Counts (No. 98)**. Beyond this point the gardens take the lead, with one hundred and ten, and one hundred and

twenty year old villas hiding in their depths. The Andrássy Street has an attraction, which is invisible from above the ground. This is the **Millennial underground**, which was put under ground, when it was built in 1896, in order to keep the look of the surface beautiful and homogenous. This was the first underground in the continent, the only older one built was in London. It served as an example for the undergrounds of other European cites.

Today it is run by the Transportation Company of Budapest, which sometimes operate special nostalgia trains, which give the almost perfect illusion of the atmosphere one hundred years ago.

Along the lengthened axis of the Andrássy Street stands the grand column of the **Millenary Monument (Ezredéves emlékmű)**.

The Heroes' Square

The Art Gallery, home of the contemporary art

On the top of the 36 metres high column stands Gabriel the Guardian Angel, the symbol of Victory, around it, upon the two, 85 metres wide and 25 metres deep, half colonnades stand the statues of Hungarian kings and the leading figures of the Hungarian independence wars. On the stone base of the statues, are reliefs about the person's life and actions. There are the allegoric bronze statues of War, Peace and Knowledge on the left hand wing, and on the right hand wing are of War, Peace and Glory on the corner pillars of the colonnade. In the middle of the square, behind the column of Gabriel are the picturesque group of statues of the conquering Magyars, with Árpád, the leading reigning prince, in the middle. The historical, romantic statue complex commemorates the thousandth year of the Hungarian state, but it was only finished in 1929. At this time the **Monument of the**

National Heroes was placed in the symbolic centre of the square, and it was given its present name, Heroes' Square (Hősök tere). Many skilful Hungarian artists worked on the monument. The statues were designed by György Zala, and the architectural elements by Albert Schikedanz.
There are two impressive buildings at the sides of the square. To the right stands the **Art Gallery (Műcsarnok)**, the exhibition hall of contemporary arts, which was built earlier. It was opened to the public, as part of the millennium celebrations in May, 1896. This classical building with rich terracotta ornaments on the bricked façade was designed by Albert Schikedanz and Fülöp Herzog with a touch of Greek style. On the left hand side of the square stands the **Museum of Fine Arts**

(Szépművészeti Múzeum). This was the last completed piece of the eclectic architecture in Hungary, with renaissance styled inner rooms. The designer was also Schikedanz, and it was finished in 1900. The Old Gallery of the Museum (already founded in the 1870s), is world famous, displaying works of Raffaello, Piombo, Breughel, Frans Hals, Rembrandt, Greco, Velázquez, Goya along with many more of the greatest artists. The graphical collection is one of the richest in Europe. The growing Egyptian collection, started at the museums foundation, is also worthwhile looking at. Behind the square is the **City Park (Városliget)**. This is one of the biggest parks in Budapest and has been a very popular excursion and relaxation place for 250 years. There are many

The Museum of Fine Arts

restaurants here, among which the Gundel's Restaurant is the oldest and most distinguished, with the most artful dishes of Hungarian cooking served in luxurious surroundings. The **Zoological Gardens**, founded in 1866 are located immediately next door to Gundel's recently refurbished restaurants. All of its major buildings are protected by preservation orders. There are hundreds of other attractions in the park, apart from the Circus and the Amusement Park, next to the Zoo, and the graceful, but rather shabby façade of the Szécheny Baths, built on an artesian well in 1877. The **Castle of Vajdahunyad** can't be omitted from here. Designed by Ignác Alpár, it was first built in the year of the millennium, and then after some years rebuilt from permanent materials. This grand building complex is a curiosity. The original version was the home of the big exhibitions' historical artefacts in 1896, and so the whole exhibition hall is a historical and exhibitional construction. It is a veritable compendium of all the architectural styles that ever took root in the history of Hungary. This unique, multi-courtyarded building is a strange mixture of Roman, Gothic, renaissance and baroque palaces, castles, towers, churches, balconies and parapets. There have been 24 elements of the complex identified by experts, which can be found somewhere in historical Hungary.

Its name comes from the part of the building (the bastion and the façade) looking over the lake (an ice-ring in winter), which portrays the tower above the gate and the hall of knights of the Vajdahunyad Castle in Transylvania. The copy of the original hall of knights can be also seen from the inside, as part of the **Agricultural Museum**, now housed here, where the visitor can walk a flight of lavish ceremonial stairs.

We are going to finish our walk at a grave, but until we get there we have the opportunity to enjoy the gnarled firs, ancient willows, giant poplars, parterres of flowers, playgrounds for children, fountains and statues. There is a walk ahead of us, until we reach the grave at the other end, the southern end of the park. There lies another villa quarter with elegant town houses along the streets between Ajtósi Dürer Street and Thököly Street. Most of them were built in the decades before the turn of the XX. century.

Only the best maps mark this little memorial site, carved from red marble, however it is quite easy to find. We just have to walk along the wide road starting at the lake, behind the Castle, the former Stefania Promenade, until the Palme House, built as one of the halls of the first national exhibition in 1885. When we pass

The Széchenyi Bath in the City Park

The Castle of Vajdahunyad

this house, there is a shadowy path leading towards a glade. At the northern side of this clearing stands the tombstone. This romantic commemoration site of the City Park has been here for almost two hundred years. Resting here lies a hardworking lawyer of Pest, Jakab T. Horváth, who said farewell to the vale of tears in 1806. He left his money to the town, and asked the town elders to bury him here, in the Park, with only one word carved on the headstone, **FUIT**, i.e. Was...

His identity has since been discovered, and this deserted area of the park is now filled with the joyful sounds of the changing generations visiting the park. This WAS was, and now it will be WILL. Practically forever, until the end of time, until the city is a city, the citizens are citizens.

Fourth walk

ÓBUDA ◆ AQUINCUM

Probably nowhere in the world do past and present rub shoulders in such close proximity as in Óbuda (Old Buda), former city of the queens of Hungary. The first interesting period in its history occurred in the second and third centuries AD This was the heyday of Aquincum, the flourishing military outpost of the Roman Empire, defending the eastern frontier from the ever increasing threat of Barbarian invasions. After the Romans abandoned this wealthy and populous city, it continued to function as an important crossing point on the Danube. First Huns, Lombards, then Avars and Slavonic tribes lived within the walls, using the villas, fortresses, baths and roads as they used the forests and the waters, as parts of their natural environments. Chronicles of subsequent centuries described the settlement as the "City of Attila", suggesting that the decaying provincial capital of the Romans was used as the administrative centre of a reigning prince, like a town.

It is always a mistake to think of history as a book in which each page contains a clearly identifiable single event, and on one page we read about the Roman Empire, and on the next about their retreat under Barbarian pressure. The material of these changes are the people, who remained here after the legions had gone. And the town lived by them, even if it didn't flourished, like when it was called Aquincum. That is how we get to the century immediately preceding the year one thousand, when the Magyars were settled in the Carpathian basin, and arrived at the rich banks of the river Danube.

The Magyars were ruled by two chieftains, who governed the seven tribes. One ruled in times of peace, the other in times of war. Árpád was the former, and Kurszán (Kursan) the latter at that time. Contemporary chronicles tell us that the amphitheatre of the old Roman legionary camp in Óbuda was Kursan's fortified stronghold, the "fortress of Kursan" where he used to receive the emissaries of foreign princes. Five hundred years after the Romans had abandoned their buildings, their walls were still standing! Árpád, too, is somehow involved with this location, if we can believe the ancient stories, and his burial place has always been believed to be somewhere nearby. It has been looked for a great deal, trying to solve the puzzle of the thousand years old descriptions, but there has been no trace of it found so far. From this time onwards the history of Óbuda is well documented. Shortly after the year 1000 the new city built on the ruins of the old Roman town became a centre for both ecclesiastical and secular power. The former was represented by the provost and the monastic orders, the latter was established by the queen and developed as a separate administrative entity for some centuries. The custom of the queens owning Óbuda was founded by Louis the Great,

Batthyány Square with the Casanova House

the Anjou king, who granted ownership of this area and its royal castle to his mother.

With only one exception, during the 150 years of Turkish invasion, when it became virtually depopulated, Óbuda has retained its importance in the history of the Capital. Today, making room for new urban development, it continues to live and flourish as it had done for centuries under the constantly changing conditions.

This town lies on the Buda side of the Danube, and we start our walk from there, maybe, departing from Batthyány Square, which itself is not without interest. In our previous walks we broadened our knowledge of Budapest, and so we can orientate ourselves with just a passing look around. Above us are the northern and eastern slopes of the Castle Hill. This hill edged the narrow land, this part of the City, called Víziváros (Water town) to the bank of he river. The square is the natural centre of this area, so it became inhabited in the early ages, but we can only see, like in the Castle, buildings representing the baroque style, preserving only little from the predecessors.

The building at **No. 3 Batthyány Square** is like this. The XVIII. century edifice has a two hundred year old baroque *frieze* depicting the four seasons, and a lovely stairway.

Its neighbour **(No. 4)** was built twenty years earlier as an inn. It used to house the **Inn to the White Cross**, where the first theatre shows were held in Buda. But it is not famous because of this, but because of a never proved anecdote. When the famous notorious seducer, Casanova lived here for quite a while, trying the curative properties of the medicinal waters of the Rácz Baths. In the meantime he fancied the daughter of a butcher, until the butcher seized his biggest cleaver and chased the would-be lover not only from his house, but from the neighbourhood. From this romantic and adventures story, it might be true that the people living here around those times were very belligerent and self-involved. Another proof of this is the story concerning the construction of **St. Anne's Church** started in the mid 1700s. To build the church according to plan, the builders found it necessary to encroach somewhat on the neighbouring property belonging to a certain Mihály Pösenbacher. This gentleman wasn't at all happy about the idea of yielding part of his land to the church, he even chased the builders away with a weapon twice. Only after a great deal of discussion could the church be built to an Italian design under the supervision of Kristóf Hamon. It was consecrated after lengthy works lasting fifty years, in 1805. The statues of Maria and Anne on the main façade, and the majority of ornaments inside the church are

from the 1760s and 1770s, but its main style is the baroque.

We now start going to the north along the old main road of the old travellers of Buda parallel to the Danube, the Main Street. We can look at some of the romantic and classical dwellings, built during the first rebuilding period of Pest, on the southern part of this street ending at the Chain Bridge, especially on its odd numbered side **(Nos. 1, 3, 5, 7, 9, 11–13, 20 Fő Street, Nos. 3, 4 Corvin Square)**. Around here stands the beautiful **church and monastery of the Capuchin Fathers (No. 30–32)**, standing in the place of a Turkish mosque built between 1703 and 1716 for the order of Father Ottó Linzi. Walking along the Fő Street we pass **the church and hospital of the St. Elizabeth nuns**. This church was also built in the place of a mosque in the 1730s, to the plans of the Franciscan Father Jakab. The hospital block was finished, and given to the nuns and the patients in 1777. Part of the hospital is a public domain, one of its wings was built from the money of the wealthy Marczibányi family in 1805, as the writing above the door recalls. The braided styled red marble coffins of sheriff István Marczibányi and his wife are placed in the crypt of the Church. The most valuable thing in the especially richly furnished church is a simple object, the stick of St. Elizabeth, healing the poor in the XVIII. century.

More to the north, under **No. 82–86. Fő Street** is another building recalling the Turkish times. Here all the descriptive marks of the invaders' architecture can be seen. The domed hall of the **King Bath (Király fürdő),** looking onto Ganz Street, was built in 1566, for the order of Arslan (Lion) pasha. Its classical wing facing Fő Street was built in 1826, by the owner, Ferenc König (King), after whom it was named.

After the many German sounding names we shall stop for a moment to talk about a part of the town history not yet discussed. After the

United Christian Army liberated Hungary from the Turks in 1686, many German settlers arrived in several waves to Pest, Buda and Óbuda. The Hungarian capital spoke and wrote in German, and the offices were in Latin by the XVIII. century. Only the pure Hungarian families used the Hungarian language at home. The majority of the middle class had German origins, and this is shown not only in the names, but also in the traditions and typical professions. Slowly things changed, and by the XIX. century the Germans became "Hungarified". It is an interesting paradox, that the soldiers, and some of the generals fighting for independence were the descendants of these Germans living in Pest and Buda.

The King Bath in the Fő Street

Those who learnt Hungarian and wanted to become Hungarians. They also changed their names to Hungarian ones. That is how Königsbad became Királyfürdő (King Bath), a small example of the changes.

Fő Street finishes at **Margaret Bridge**, the second permanent bridge over the Danube. We take a little walk up on the **Hill of Roses (Rózsadomb)**, one of the most elegant quarters of Budapest. This elegance however is not exactly typical of the part we are heading towards, although some villas and town-houses can also be found here (these are much higher up and on the south-west slope of the hill). The person who this district was named after used to live at what is now **No. 14. Mecset Street**, at that time there were no houses or streets there. This is Baba Gül, the Turkish saint, whose grave is the most western pilgrimage site of the Muslims, who remained, after the Turks had to give up their boundaries in Hungary, alone, here along the Danube.

Baba Gül, or the Father of the Roses, belonged to the first generation occupying Buda, and set up his monastery as the head of the Order of the dervishes of Bektas on the empty green slope facing the Danube. According to the legend, he planted beautiful roses all around the building. This is where the name of the hill came from, from the rose garden of the dervish, who died and was also buried here.

The ***türbe*** of **Baba Gül** is an octagonal shaped chapel, carved from stone, its interior ornamented with the typical ornaments of Turkish architecture, donkey-back shaped arches and the ornamented half cupola. In the middle lies the symbolic grave of the dervish chief with old and new presents of the pilgrims, coloured carpets, flags, ribbons. The chapel was built by the pasha conquering Buda, Jahja Zade Mohomet, between 1543 and 1548.

The northern slopes of the next hill, Szemlőhegy, built together with Rózsadomb,

The chapel of Baba Gül

has a border with Óbuda. The Town of the Queens starts only a kilometre away from the grave of the Father of the Roses. Beyond the crossing of **Nagyszombat Street**, there stand the walls of a great arena, causing the Lajos Street to alter its course. These are Roman walls, the remains of the **amphitheatre** of one of Aquincum's districts inhabited by legions. Its ground plan is oval shaped with the major axis being ninety metres. The ring is bigger than the ring of the Coliseum in Rome! It has cast walls and the arcades were made with the so called fish bone structure. The walls are held by huge stone pillars. Its capacity approached 10–12 thousand persons. Aquincum used to be a big city with a popular amphitheatre. The later

fortress of the Hungarian leader was built in the middle of the II. century AD.

Approaching the most northern bridge on the Danube, we can discover the former **Trinity Church and Cloister** with its strong walls on the hill to the left. The site was chosen by the Count Zichy family, the owners of Óbuda, as their burial place, and they started to build the Church in 1744 under the supervision of Johann Entzenhoffer. It was ready by 1760, but not long after that, the Jesuits had to hand the building over to the military treasury, when Joseph II. dissolved the orders in Hungary.

Ladies with umbrellas, created by Imre Varga, on the Fő Square of Óbuda

The Town Hall of Óbuda

Today it is owned by the new ages collection of the **History Museum of Budapest**. Within the exhibition we can take a closer look at the memories of past actions and history, which we met during our walks.

To the left, before the bridge head lies the **Town of the Queens**. This is the part of Óbuda, where we can find most traces of its past. The baroque tower of the **Roman Catholic Parish Church** protrudes from the rows of the other houses. The whole church is built in baroque style, in 1744–1749. Its architect was called György Paur. According to the archaeologists, in its place used to stand the main church of the Town of the Queens, which is mentioned in the

The Zichy Castle in Óbuda

The stairway of the Zichy Castle

medieval chronicles as the Margit Chapel. The builders are the Count Zichys, who also used this site as their burial place. The rich statue ornaments of the Church and the statues standing in front of it **(St. Florian and St. John of Nepumuk)** are identified as the works of Károly Bebo, who created a popular style of architecture in the middle of the XVIII. century. The **Parish House**, standing on the corner of the church's square and Lajos Street **(No. 168 Lajos Street)** evokes the century of the baroque little town. It was built in 1756. Near here **(No. 158)** stands a multi-storey house. It has been rebuilt many times since the Middle Ages, the last time was in 1774. The **Brewery (Serfőzőház)**, as it was called after one of its owners living here of this profession, is one of

the oldest houses in Óbuda. There are also some other equally old houses here, especially in the **Mókus Street (Squirrel Street),** starting behind the church. There is **No. 2** on the corner, built in classical style around 1840, and **No. 22**, standing here since 1820. The latter famous, almost one hundred year-old **Kéhli Restaurant**, in the old style of the famous friendly restaurants in Óbuda awaiting the visitor with fine local wines and music. The **Dugovics Titusz Square** is surrounded by some of these old buildings.

There is another church also in the neighbourhood, built in 1820, for the Jewish people of the district, who for a long time used

Fő Square, Óbuda

to be in the majority around here. The **Synagogue of Óbuda (163. Lajos Street)** was built in classical style by András Landherr, hoping to reach monumentality.

On the other side of the bridge head, northwards of the old town centre, now separated from the synagogue stands the former **castle of the Zichys**, the centre of their lands (of course, the separation didn't exist until the Árpád Bridge was finished in 1950, it was the youngest bridge until 1996, when the Lágymányosi Bridge was built).

In order to get there we have to walk through the long corridors under the Árpád Bridge, where we can look at the exhibition of the ancient **Roman ruins** found during the construction of the bridge. There is also a museum, where the restored ruins of the excavated **military baths** can be seen. These were a huge building, their area was 120x140 metres. Nowhere else in Aquincum have so intact floor heating systems been found, this very popular system heated the hot, lukewarm and cool pools, and their servicing buildings with community rooms, and supplied fountains, and ornaments made from mosaic with water.

The **Fő Square (Main Square)** is the centre of the northern part around the bridge head. Its birth was provoked by the **Zichy Castle (1. Fő Square)**, standing on the courtyards of the baroque side buildings. Its façade and the balconies are memories from the wealthy past, like the main stairway ornamented with richly carved figures and balustrade railing. The statues are the work of Károly Bebo, and the building is a masterpiece of János Henrik Jaeger. It was completed in the middle of the XVIII. century when it was handed over to the owner, Count Miklós Zichy.

The Fő Square is the old, but not the oldest administration centre of Óbuda, with pretty old houses **(No. 4, 5)** and lots of restaurants, imitating the style of the old Óbuda. Of course,

they can cook well, giving a delicious luncheon to the hungry passer-by.

We have to walk two kilometres from here to get to the large excavation site of the **civilian town of Aquincum**, and dive into the past, until the earliest reaches of our time travel.

The town from the ancient times was created in the I. century by craftsmen, who moved down from Gellért Hill, after the legions had arrived here and were known as the Eraviscuses. This Celtic tribe had to look after the soldiers and accompaniments stationed here (six thousand soldiers and the minimum of two thousand settlers coming with the first wave in 89 AD). This was a huge new market and offered a wealthy lifestyle, and these people serving the Romans year by year came to consider themselves Roman and accept their culture, worship their gods and marry with there sons and daughters. They became Romans, as had happened in other parts of the world, thousands and thousands of kilometres away from here. During the rule of Hadrianus (124 AD) this already town-like settlement became a municipium, an official town, this is when the free people of the settlement became Roman citizens. Septimus Severus Ceasar gave it the rank of colony in 194 AD, and then the city enjoyed autonomy, it could rule its own territory of sixty kilometres radius.

The "industrial" settlement of the II. century flourished in the III. century as a "resort" richly endowed with all the luxuries the age could offer like baths, lavish villas and two coliseums. The number of its estimated inhabitants became more than ten thousand. As the threat of the Barbarian invasion was increasing, the focus of activity gradually shifted to the military settlement, and by the beginning of the V. century, the civilian town had become deserted.

Aquincum, "wide water", covering the area of 400x500 metres was girdled by a wall and a ditch. Its **four town gates** opened to the four

The ruin town of Aquincum, including the Museum

points of the compass (two of which were excavated and can be seen on the site), and were connected by two roads. At the cross-roads of these, was the **Forum**, where the buildings of administration, the **Church of Capitolium**, the **Basilica** (building of justice) and the **Curia** (building of the council) used to stand. The **Central Public Bath** was also situated along here, although there were smaller baths in each district, and of course in the military camp too. The **Market Hall** opened from the main street, there were also shops, churches and public wells, including some very elegant ones. There was no lack of trade nor comfort (which here mainly means the perfect water supply and the canals) nor pomp. Several of the floor mosaics of the houses are displayed in the exhibition, which were created in the period of prosperity of the III. century.

The excavations of Aquincum begun in the 1880s, and are still continuing today, only the **central area of the town** is on display. The **Aquincum Museum** displaying some of the treasures discovered, from the statues, to the carved stones in its rooms and its open balcony, is more than one hundred years old, awaiting the passing visitor and ready to show some fragments of the way of life that ended 1500 years ago.

We, who walk along the most important stages of the previous centuries, can see the ceremonial moment of birth together with the grandiose steps of the constant changes here, in Aquincum. These changes, and the final result of the story and of our walks, have created here, in the valley of the Danube, one of the most beautiful capitals of Europe, Budapest.

SZENTENDRE

Slightly bigger than a little village (the part which is visited by tourists), however it is obvious from the first glance, that this is a town. It is only half an hours travelling distance away from Budapest by any public transport, but those who come here can gain an overall view of the countryside of Hungary. This is Szentendre, the fairy tale town along the Danube, which is not only famous for its museums, but for being a museum itself in this picturesque setting of the surrounding hills. The ancient village was founded in the XI. century. It got its name from the Guardian Angel of its church, András (Endre). After several quiet centuries, the XIV. century brought a change to its status, and it became a royal estate with privileges. The one hundred and fifty years of the Turkish occupation ended with its total desertion. But its rebirth also was connected to this period. The victorious Christian armies set off to the south to liberate the southern countries, and the Serbs under Turkish occupation cherished them. But around 1690, the dice turned, and the Serbs, afraid of the vengeance of the Muslims, fled to Hungary. About forty thousand families, which is more than a hundred thousand people. This is the time, when the Tabán got its new inhabitants, when the Serbs built churches in Pest, and when they moved into the deserted villages and towns. A total number of six thousand people moved to Szentendre.

Since, they all thought this was only their temporary home, they built their shelters,

▷ *The pedestrian zone in Szentendre*

Houses of the Fő Square in Szentendre

houses and churches in different quarters, **mehalas**, keeping separated the peoples of different regions. After a few decades it became apparent that this was going to be their final home, their cradle and their grave. Thanks to the Danube, it became a trade town, with rich merchants and craftsmen, who soon had the opportunity to rebuild their houses and churches in a more durable manner. There were as many Orthodox churches, as there were mehalas, they still dot the area of the old city with their heads. Their golden age was the XVIII. century. After that, the decay starts. The development stops, and everything changes. There is no money, no will, the dynamism of the community also fades. There were no new buildings, and thanks to this, Szentendre has mainly stayed the same as it was at the dawn of the XIX. century or a even a little earlier. An atmospheric and romantic memorial of its heydays. It was discovered in modern times by the Hungarian artists, painters, sculptors who settled here, and museums, too, which are well known both inside and outside the country. Probably the most famous is the **Museum of Margit Kovács**, the uncrowned queen of the XX. century Hungarian ceramics. Her collection (under **No. 1 György Vastagh Street**), fills up a beautiful XVIII. century Serbian house from the

▷ *The Cross of the Merchants and the Blagovestenszka Church*

The "streets" around the Castle Hill can only be discovered on foot

cellar to the loft. Its equal is the **Ferenczy Museum** on the **Fő tér (Main Square)**, which displays the valued works of the four generations of the Ferenczy family.

First we have to stop here, on the Fő Square for a minute to stare at the best known face of Szentendre. Here houses queue close to each other in the Jenő Dumtsa Street towards Buda, and in the Bogdányi Street towards the North. Almost every one is either a restaurant or a shop offering valuable goods. The streets coming from the Danube bank look similar, with houses radiating many colours, hidden in the crooked streets. On the **Fő Square**, there is another Pravoslovnic church, the **Blagovestenska** (addressed to the greetings of the angels), bearing baroque and rococo styles, which was built in the middle of the XVIII. century. The rich carvings on the iconostasis and its baroque paintings were the work of Mihály Zsivkovics, a Hungarian-Serb. The influences of the one hundred and fifty years can be observed in these works, which were lived through by the Serbs that lived here, on this island in the sea of Hungarians.

Around the square there are well kept houses, all from the most prosperous years of the XVIII. century. Also from this period is the **Memorial Cross** in the middle of the little square, which was erected in thanks for the end of the Black Death, by the Serbian Privileged Merchants' Company in 1763. It is not a statue, like the one in the Buda Castle, for example, because the orthodox religion does not permit such things, but this cast iron cross, standing on a red marble base ornamented by a garland of icons around it, makes this memorial unique.

Opposite the Blagovestenska church, there is a narrow lane leading up to the cobbled **Church Square (Templom tér)**, the highest point of the town kernel. From behind the thick parapet we can enjoy the beautiful view over the town and the Danube. The varying streets, the tightly

The Parish Church of Szentendre on the Castle Hill

packed buildings with their overlapping roofs, looking like a red cavalcade at the edge of the Danube doted with some green gardens.

As far back as the Middle Ages there has been a church on the hill, a catholic fortress church, at the time when the area was called the Town of St. Endre. Today's parish church is the **church of St. John the Baptist**, which was built upon the original walls in the XVIII. century. Its furniture, the altars and the baroque statues are from the 1700s, as well as the richly ornamented rococo altar.

From here, our other destinations, the churches of the mehalas, and some romantic houses can clearly be seen. We can recognise the **Churches of Csiprovacska, Pozsarevacska and Perobrazsenszka**, and the other memorable, or just pretty places in this little old Serbian town, offering thousands of colourful attractions.

In the valley of the hills behind the town, easily reached by town busses, is an interesting site of the fairy tale town. This is the **largest outdoor village museum**, the Skanzen in Hungary, which was opened in 1974. Its designers tried to represent all of the Hungarian national architectural styles of each of the different

... those charming roof tops

areas, and display them in separate villages. The originals of the houses, buildings and machines were carefully taken apart and carried here from where they had no future any more and were then reassembled here. The old Hungarian crafts are also shown and taught on summer Sundays for those, who are interested, including many children, who come to camp around here and have very little idea of the beautiful secrets of their ancestors' profession. Those of you who walked along these walks with us, also visiting the skanzen (officially called the **Szabadtéri Néprajzi Múzeum**), now, closing the book and finishing our tour, can say, that you not only got to know Budapest better, but also became a bit more familiar with the whole country, Hungary. Maybe even a little closer, than you were expecting at the beginning. And you might want to carry on with the walks, making your own discoveries. Because now you know, that what you know is hardly anything compared with what you could know about this little world, thought to be exotic, but really a part of Europe since long ago.